Quick and Easy, Proven Recipes

South-East Asian Food

Publisher & Creative Director: Nick Wells
Senior Project Editor: Catherine Taylor
Art Director: Mike Spender
Layout Design: Jane Ashley
Digital Design & Production: Chris Herbert

Special thanks to Esme Chapman and Frances Bodiam.

This is a **FLAME TREE** Book

FLAME TREE PUBLISHING
Crabtree Hall, Crabtree Lane
Fulham, London SW6 6TY
United Kingdom
www.flametreepublishing.com

First published 2014

14 16 18 17 15
1 3 5 4 2

ISBN: 978-1-78361-246-8

Printed in Singapore

All images © Flame Tree Publishing Ltd, except the following which are courtesy Shutterstock.com and the following photographers: 9t Elnur; 9b Joerg Beuge; 11b, 13b zkruger; 12b johnfoto18; 13t happystock; 14t JPL Designs; 15 JIANG HONGYAN; 16 foodiepics; 17t keng88; 17b Gayvoronskaya_Yana; 18t Sunny Forest; 18b neil langan; 19t Africa Studio; 19b leungchopan; 20t QiuJu Song; 23b Wiratchai wansamngam.

Quick and Easy, Proven Recipes

South-East Asian Food

**FLAME TREE
PUBLISHING**

Contents

Essentials

South-East Asian food is both distinctive and delicious. With original flavour combinations and varied ingredients, there is something to suit every taste. Before you get stuck into the recipes that this book has to offer, use this chapter to brush up on your ingredients basics. Covering both fresh and store-cupboard ingredients commonly used in South-East Asian Cooking, you will soon know your ginger from your galangal and your shrimp paste from your oyster sauce!

Fresh Ingredients

In all Asian cooking, the basic philosophy of balance is the same, where the freshest produce is combined with the flavours of dried, salted and fermented ingredients, preserves and condiments. Most ingredients are now available in ordinary supermarkets and a few of the more unusual ones in Asian or Chinese groceries and markets.

∾ Aubergines – Chinese aubergines are thinner, with a more delicate flavour, than the Mediterranean variety. They are used in many savoury dishes and in Thailand, some varieties are eaten raw with a dip or sauce.

∾ Mushrooms – Oyster mushrooms with their subtle flavour and delicate, almost slippery texture often feature in Chinese cooking. Now cultivated, they are widely available. The colour of the fan-shaped cap gives the mushroom its name, although they can also be pink or yellow as well as grey. Tear into long triangular segments, following the lines of the gills, and cook the smaller ones whole. Shiitake mushrooms were originally Oriental, but they are now grown all over the world. They are more often used dried in Chinese cooking, but may also be used fresh – the caps have a strong flavour and are generally sliced and the stalks discarded. Cook the mushrooms gently for a short time, as they may toughen if overcooked. Straw mushrooms are sometimes known as double mushrooms because that is exactly what they look like: two mushrooms that grow end to end. They are small and pale brown with a pale-coloured stem.

~ Baby Sweetcorn – These tiny, tender cobs of sweetcorn, about 7.5 cm/3 inches long, are crunchy and sweet. When buying, make sure that they are bright yellow with no brown patches, firm and crisp.

~ Bamboo Shoots – Bamboo shoots are young, creamy-coloured, conical-shaped shoots of edible bamboo plants. They add a crunchy texture and clean, mild flavour and are sometimes available in Chinese groceries, as well as vacuum-packed or canned in most supermarkets. If you buy the latter, transfer them to a container of water once they have been opened. If you change the water daily, they will keep for up to five days in the refrigerator.

~ Beansprouts – These are the shoots of the mung bean and are readily available prepacked in the vegetable section of most supermarkets. They add a wonderfully crisp texture when added to stir-fries and take only a minute or two to cook. Ideally, the brown root should be removed from each sprout and discarded, however, this is time consuming, but improves the appearance of the dish.

~ Mangetout – These tender green pea pods with flat, barely formed peas have a deliciously crisp texture. To prepare them for cooking, simply top and tail, pulling away any string from the edges.

~ Yard-long Beans – Although unrelated to French beans, they are similar in appearance, but about four times longer. As they grow, they start

Fresh Ingredients

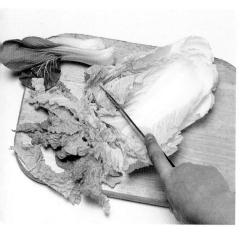

to curl and are often sold in looped bunches. Two varieties exist: a pale green type and a much darker, thinner variety. They are very popular and may be found in great quantities in Chinese markets. The Cantonese often cook them with black beans or fermented bean curd and in Sichuan, they are deep-fried. Store in a plastic bag in the refrigerator for up to four days. To prepare, cut into lengths and use in exactly the same way as French beans.

- Bok Choi – Also known as pak choi, the most common variety has long, slightly ridged white stems like celery and large, oval thick dark green leaves. It has a mild, fresh, slightly peppery taste and needs very little cooking. Choose smaller ones if possible, as they are more tender. Store in the bottom of the refrigerator.

- Chinese Mustard Cabbage – Also known as gaai choi, these mustard plants are similar in appearance to cabbages. The whole leaf is eaten, usually shredded into soups and stir-fries to which they add a fresh astringent flavour.

- Chinese Leaves – Also known as Chinese cabbage, Chinese leaves look like a large, tightly packed lettuce with crinkly, pale green leaves. It adds a crunchy texture to stir-fries.

- Chinese Kale – This green vegetable is popular in Thai cuisine. It has an almost earthy and slightly bitter taste and is usually served blanched and accompanied by oyster sauce. When buying, look for firm stems and fresh, dark green leaves. Store in the bottom drawer of the refrigerator for up to four days.

ᖳ **Water Spinach** – This is widely grown throughout Asia and is unrelated to ordinary spinach. The leaves are elongated and tender and the stems fine and delicate. Water spinach requires minimal cooking. It is cooked in the same way as spinach, either steamed, stir-fried or added to soups.

ᖳ **Chinese Celery** – Unlike the Western variety, Chinese celery stalks are thin, hollow and very crisp and range from pure white to dark green. Used as both a herb and a vegetable, Chinese celery is often stir-fried or used in soups and braised dishes.

ᖳ **Basil** – Holy basil with small, dark leaves and purple stalks is frequently used in Thai cooking, although sweet basil, more easily obtainable here, may be used instead.

ᖳ **Coriander** – Fresh coriander is the most popular fresh herb used in Thai cooking. It has an appearance similar to flat-leaf parsley, but has a pungent, slightly citrus flavour. Leaves, stems and roots are all used, so buy in big fresh bunches if possible.

ᖳ **Curry Leaves** – The shiny leaves of the curry tree (*Murraya koenigii*) are important in Indian and South-East Asian cuisine, used much like bay leaves are in the West. They can be crushed using a pestle and mortar or fried in hot oil to release their nutty fragrance, or can be torn into shreds or placed in whole at the start of cooking.

Fresh Ingredients

~ Chillies – There are many different kinds of chillies and generally, the smaller they are the more fierce the heat. Red chillies are generally milder than green ones because they sweeten as they become riper. The tiny, slender tapering red or green bird's eye (or Thai) chillies are very hot and pungent. Cooks often include the seeds in cooking, but to moderate the heat, scrape out and discard the seeds.

~ Tamarind – This adds an essential sour taste to many dishes. It is extracted from the pods as a sticky brown pulp, which is soaked to make tamarind water.

~ Garlic – This popular seasoning flavours much of Asian cooking. In Thailand, garlic heads are smaller and thinner skinned, so they are often used whole as well as finely chopped or crushed. Choose firm garlic, preferably with a pinkish tinge and store in a cool, dry place, but not in the refrigerator.

~ Shallots – Small, mild-flavoured members of the onion family, shallots have coppery-coloured skins. Use them in the same way as onions, or thinly slice and deep-fry to use as a garnish.

~ Spring Onions – Long, slender spring onions are the immature bulbs of yellow onions. They are frequently used in stir fries, as they cook within minutes.

~ Ginger – Fresh root ginger has a pungent, spicy, fresh taste. It is usually peeled, then finely chopped or grated – vary the amount of ginger used to suit your own taste.

For just a hint, slice thickly and add to the dish when cooking, then remove just before serving. Fresh ginger is infinitely preferable to the powdered variety, which loses its flavour rapidly. Fresh ginger should feel firm when you buy it. If you have more than you need it can be used within a week. Store it in the freezer as it can be grated from frozen.

ᵔ Galangal – This is a rhizome, called laos or ka in Thailand. It is similar to ginger, but the skin is a pinkish colour and the flavour more complex and mellow. Peel it thinly and slice or grate the flesh. When sliced, it can be kept in an airtight container in the refrigerator for up to two weeks. If unavailable, ginger is an acceptable substitute.

ᵔ Krachai – Also known as lesser ginger, this is smaller and more spicy than either ginger or galangal. It can be bought fresh in Oriental food shops or dried in small packets.

ᵔ Chinese Keys – Despite its name, this root vegetable is often used in Thai cuisine and rarely in Chinese. It is a member of the ginger family, with an aromatic sweet flavour that goes well in Thai curries.

ᵔ Lotus Root – This is the underwater rhizome of the lotus flower and has a lacy appearance when sliced and a sweet, crunchy flavour. Fresh lotus root takes about two hours to cook, so it is worth considering using canned lotus root instead. It is used in soups and deep-fried, stir-fried and braised dishes.

Fresh Ingredients

❧ Mooli – Also known as daikon or white radish, these look like smooth, white parsnips (they come from the same family as the radish). They have a peppery, fresh taste and are often used in salads, peeled and thinly sliced or grated. They can also be cooked, but because they have a high water content, they should be salted to extract some of the liquid, then rinsed well and steamed or boiled. They are often carved into beautiful and intricate shapes as a table decoration or garnish.

❧ Water Chestnuts – These are bulbs of an Asian water plant that look like and are a similar size to chestnuts. When peeled, the inner flesh is very crisp. Some Oriental grocers sell them fresh, although canned, either whole or sliced, are almost as good.

❧ Kaffir Lime Leaves – Dark green, smooth, glossy leaves, these come from the kaffir lime tree and are highly sought after for Thai cooking. They add a distinctive citrus flavour to curries, soups and sauces. Buy them from larger supermarkets and Oriental grocery shops and keep them in a sealed polythene bag in the freezer. Lime zest can be used as an alternative.

❧ Lemon Grass – These look a bit like spring onions, but are much tougher. The stems should be bashed to release the lemony flavour during cooking, then removed before serving. Alternatively, peel away the outer layers and chop the heart very finely.

- **Durian** – This large, spiky-skinned tropical fruit has such an unpleasantly strong aroma that it is banned from public transport and hotels in Bangkok. It is expensive to buy a whole fruit, but you can sometimes buy frozen packs of skinless pieces of fruit.

- **Mango** – This sweet, fragrant, juicy fruit is a delicious addition to many Asian dishes, sweet or savoury, whether salads, salsas or stir-fries. To test ripeness, press each end of the fruit firmly – if it yields to the pressure then it is ready; if not, it can be left to ripen in a sunny place.

- **Papaya** – Also called pawpaw, the unripe green flesh of this tropical fruit is often used in Thai cooking. It ripens to a deep orange colour and is delicious sliced and served as a dessert.

- **Tofu** – Tofu or bean curd has been used as an ingredient in Thai and Chinese cooking for over 1,000 years. Made from yellow soya beans, which are soaked, ground and briefly cooked, tofu is very rich in protein and low in calories. Because of its bland taste it is ideal cooked with stronger flavourings. It is usually available in two types: a soft variety known as silken tofu that can be used for soups and desserts, and a firm, solid white block, which can be cubed or sliced and included in stir-frying and braising. Also available is smoked tofu, which is a seasoned bean curd. When using, cut into the required size with care and do not stir too much when cooking otherwise it will disintegrate and lose its texture; it simply needs to be heated through.

Fresh Ingredients

Store-cupboard Ingredients

There are many dry, canned and preserved ingredients that are essential to creating the full flavour of Asian dishes, not to mention the range of rice and noodles that will soak up all the wonderful juices and sauces.

❧ **Beans and Pulses** – Many beans and pulses (dried and canned) are used in Asian cooking. For example, black beans are small, black soya beans that may also be known as salted black beans, as they have been fermented with salt and spices. Sold loose in Chinese groceries, but also available canned, they have a rich flavour and are often used with ginger and garlic with which they have a particular affinity.

Adzuki beans are often used in desserts, sweetened to make red bean paste or combined with other ingredients for dishes such as 'Adzuki Porridge'.

❧ **Cashew Nuts** – These milky-flavoured nuts have a crunchy texture and are often used whole or chopped in Chinese cooking, particularly as an ingredient in chicken dishes.

❧ **Mushrooms** – Many sorts of dried mushrooms are used in Asian cooking. Cloud ear (black fungus) mushrooms need soaking in warm water for about 20 minutes before use.

They have a subtle, mild flavour and are highly regarded for their colour and gelatinous flavour. Dried shiitake mushrooms have a very strong flavour and are used in small quantities. After soaking, the hard stalks are usually discarded or added to stock.

∽ Chillies – Dried red chillies are a common and popular ingredient used throughout much of South-East Asia. The drying process concentrates the flavour, making them more fiery. Look for dried chillies with a bright red colour and a pungent aroma. If stored in a sealed container, they will keep almost indefinitely. Chilli oil is made from crushed dried chillies or whole fresh chillies and is used as both a seasoning and a dipping condiment. Chilli powder is made from dried red chillies and is usually mixed with other spices and seasonings, ranging from mild and aromatic to very hot – always check the jar before using. Chilli bean sauce is a thick, dark paste made from soya beans, chillies and other spicy seasonings and is very hot. Seal the jar after use and store in the refrigerator.

∽ Szechuan Peppercorns – This small reddish spice has a distinct, woody flavour and is more fragrantly spicy than hot. It is one of the spices in Chinese five-spice powder. Also known as fargara and Chinese pepper, Szechuan peppercorns are used extensively in Szechuan cooking. Unrelated to peppers, they are the dried berries of a shrub and have a slight numbing effect on the tongue.

Store-cupboard Ingredients

Cardamom – A spice with medicinal properties, cardamom is used in curries and rice dishes. Cardamom pods come in green and black varieties.

Star Anise – This is an eight-pointed, star-shaped pod with a strong aniseed flavour. It is added whole to many Chinese dishes whilst they cook, but is usually removed before serving. It is also a vital ingredient in Chinese five-spice powder.

Cloves – Cloves have a distinctive sweet, spicy and peppery flavour. They can be used whole or ground and should be used in moderation due to their strength.

Coriander – Ground coriander is made from coriander seeds and has an almost sweet, spicy, fresh flavour. You can buy it ready ground or instead toast whole seeds in the oven and grind them yourself.

Cumin – This strong spice adds warmth and earthiness to recipes, and comes ground or in seed form.

Turmeric – This mild flavoured spice adds a bright yellow hue to foods. Although it can sometimes be bought fresh, it is most often used in its dried powdered form.

Sugar – Added in small quantities to many savoury dishes, sugar balances the flavour of a dish, and gives a shiny appearance to the sauces. Thai palm sugar comes in large lumps or slabs, which need to be bashed with a mallet, to break into smaller pieces.

Coconut Milk – Rich, creamy coconut milk is extracted from the white flesh of the nut. It can be bought in cans or made by adding boiling water to a sachet of coconut powder. Sometimes an opaque, white cream rises to the top of canned coconut milk and solidifies. You should shake the can before opening. If the milk is stored in an airtight container in the refrigerator it will last for up to three days, however, it does not freeze well. Occasionally, freshly made coconut milk may be bought from Oriental groceries. It is often used in Thai cooking, especially in curries and may also be used in desserts.

Creamed Coconut – Made from coconut oils and other fats, this comes in a hard, white block. It is not a substitute for coconut milk and is usually added at the end of cooking, to thicken a sauce, or to add coconut flavour to a finished dish.

Wonton Wrappers – Also called wonton skins, wonton wrappers are egg and flour pastry-like wrappings that can be stuffed then fried, steamed or added to soups. Fresh ones may be stored for about five days in the refrigerator if kept wrapped in clingfilm.

Noodles – There are many types of noodles used in Thai and Chinese cuisine. The most popular include cellophane noodles – also known as glass noodles – that are white and become transparent when cooked. Made from ground mung beans, they are never served on their own, but are added to soups or are deep-fried and used as a garnish. Egg noodles can be bought fresh, but the dried ones, which come in fine and

Store-cupboard Ingredients

medium, are just as good. Generally, flat noodles are used in soups and round ones for stir-fries. Rice noodles are fine, opaque noodles made from rice flour and are also called rice sticks. They are common in southern China, as it is the rice growing area of the country. Wheat is the primary grain in northern China and is made into noodles without egg. These noodles are sold in compressed square packages and bundles. Yifu noodles are round, yellow noodles, woven in a round cake and are often sold precooked.

∾ Rice – Long-grain white rice is the most commonly used rice for serving with many of the dishes in this book. Glutinous rice is a short-grain variety often used in desserts. It is sometimes referred to as sticky rice. Thai Jasmine or Fragrant rice is a long-grain rice from Thailand with an aromatic and subtle flavour.

∾ Rice Paper – This is made from a mixture of rice flour, water and salt, which is rolled out by machine until it is paper-thin and dried. It comes in round or triangular pieces which can be softened by placing between two damp tea towels and are then used to make spring rolls.

∾ Rice Vinegars – There are several varieties: white vinegar is clear and mild; red vinegar is slightly sweet and quite salty and is often used as a dipping sauce; black vinegar is very rich, yet mild and sweet vinegar is very thick, dark-coloured and flavoured with star anise.

∾ Rice Wine – Often used in Chinese cooking in both marinades and sauces, rice wine is made from

glutinous rice and has a rich, mellow taste. Do not confuse rice wine with sake, which is the Japanese version, as it is very different. Pale dry sherry is a good substitute for rice wine.

❧ Sesame Oil – This is a thick, dark-golden to brown aromatic oil that is made from sesame seeds. It is rarely used in frying, as it has a low smoke-point, but when it is, it should be combined with another oil. It is often added to a finished dish in small quantities.

❧ Sesame Paste – Sesame paste is a rich, very creamy brown paste made from sesame seeds, however, it is not the same as tahini paste from the Middle-East. If unavailable, use smooth peanut butter, which has a similar texture.

❧ Sesame Seeds – These are the dried seeds of the sesame herb. Unhulled, the seeds may be dull white to black in colour, but once the hull is removed, the seeds are a creamy-white colour. Sesame seeds are often used as a garnish or as a light coating to add crunch to food. Toast them first, to intensify their flavour, by shaking over heat in a dry frying pan until the seeds are lightly coloured.

❧ Groundnut Oil – Also known as peanut oil, this has a mild, nutty flavour. Because it can be heated to high temperatures, it is ideal for both stir-frying and deep-frying.

❧ Soy Sauce – Both light and dark soy sauce feature frequently in Chinese and Thai cooking. It is made from a mixture of soya beans, flour and water, which is fermented together and allowed to age. The resulting liquid that is then distilled is soy sauce. Light soy sauce has a lighter colour and is more salty than the dark variety. It is often labelled as 'superior soy'. Dark soy sauce is aged for longer and the colour is almost black. Its flavour is stronger and is slightly thicker than light soy sauce. Confusingly, this is labelled in Thai and Chinese food shops as 'Soy Superior sauce'. It is also possible to buy a mushroom-flavoured soy sauce, which is made by the infusion of dry straw mushrooms, and a shrimp-flavoured soy sauce.

- **Hoisin Sauce** – This is a thick, dark brownish-red sauce, which is sweet, tangy and spicy. Made from soya beans, salt, flour, sugar, vinegar, chilli, garlic and sesame oil, it may be used as a dip, in 'red-cooking' and as a baste for roasted meats.

- **Nam Pla Fish Sauce** – This is a golden brown, thin sauce with a salty flavour and is made from salted and fermented fresh fish, usually anchovies. It is used in Thai cooking in much the same way as soy sauce is used in Chinese cooking. The fishy aroma is almost unpleasant when the bottle is opened, but this mellows when mixed with other ingredients, adding a unique Thai flavour.

- **Oyster Sauce** – This is a thick, brown sauce made from oysters cooked in soy sauce. It has a wonderfully rich, but not fishy flavour, as this disappears during processing. Often used as a condiment, it is also one of the most used ingredients in southern Chinese cuisine.

- **Shrimp Paste** – Made from puréed, fermented salted shrimps, this is popular in Thai cooking and adds a distinctive fishy flavour. There is also a Chinese version, which has an even stronger aroma. Use both sparingly as they can be strong. Dried salted shrimps are also available, which are sometimes used as a seasoning in stir-fries. They should be soaked first in warm water, then puréed in a blender or made into a paste by grinding with a pestle and mortar.

- **Yellow Bean Sauce** – This thick, aromatic sauce is made with fermented yellow beans, flour and salt and adds a distinctive flavour to sauces. It is popular in Chinese cooking.

- **Plum Sauce** – As the name suggests, plum sauce is made from plums that are simmered together with vinegar, sugar, ginger, chilli and other spices.

- **Thai Curry Paste** – Red curry paste is a strongly flavoured spicy paste made mainly from dried red chillies that are blended with other spices and herbs. There is also green curry paste, which is hotter and made from fresh green chillies.

- **Thousand-year-old Eggs** – Fresh duck eggs are often preserved in brine, which seeps into the shell, making the whites salty and the yolks firm and orange-coloured. Thousand-year-old eggs are preserved in a mixture of clay, fine ash and salt. The whites of the eggs turn a translucent black and the yolks a grey-green colour after a year or so, hence their name. Unopened eggs can be kept for many months.

- **Cassia** – This is the bark taken from a cassia or laurel tree and is dark brown and flat in shape. It is similar, but slightly less subtle than cinnamon.

- **Bird's Nest** – This very expensive delicacy is literally a bird's nest made from the spittle of a swallow. It is harvested from caves or special nesting houses and can occasionally be found in Chinese food shops. It is sold as a crunchy jelly that is often added to sauces, soups and extravagant stuffings and is an acquired taste. Since it is dried, it can be stored in a dry place for several years. To use, it should be soaked overnight in cold water, then simmered for 20 minutes in fresh water.

Store-cupboard Ingredients

Snacks  Starters

Tasty snacks and starter-sized dishes abound throughout South-East Asia, and whether you are looking for a quick lunch or introduction to an exotic feast, this chapter is sure to hold a recipe that ticks the box. Guests will love the richly flavoured Shredded Duck in Lettuce Leaves, whilst the Vegetable Thai Spring Rolls are so crispy and scrumptious you might need to cook up two batches at a time!

Mixed Satay Sticks

Serves 4

12 large raw prawns
350 g/12 oz beef rump steak
1 tbsp lemon juice
1 garlic clove, peeled and crushed
pinch salt
2 tsp soft dark brown sugar
1 tsp ground cumin
1 tsp ground coriander
$^1/_4$ tsp ground turmeric
1 tbsp groundnut oil
fresh coriander leaves, to garnish

For the spicy peanut sauce:

1 shallot, peeled and very
finely chopped
1 tsp demerara sugar
50 g/2 oz creamed
coconut, chopped
pinch chilli powder
1 tbsp dark soy sauce
125 g/4 oz crunchy peanut butter

Preheat the grill on high just before required. Soak eight bamboo skewers in cold water for at least 30 minutes. Peel the prawns, leaving the tails on. Using a sharp knife, remove the black vein along the back of the prawns. Cut the beef into 1 cm/$^1/_2$ inch wide strips. Place the prawns and beef in separate bowls and sprinkle each with $^1/_2$ tablespoon of the lemon juice.

Mix together the garlic, a pinch of salt, sugar, cumin, coriander, turmeric and groundnut oil to make a paste. Lightly brush over the prawns and beef. Cover and place in the refrigerator to marinate for at least 30 minutes, but for longer if possible.

Meanwhile, make the sauce. Pour 125 ml/4 fl oz of water into a small saucepan, add the shallot and sugar and heat gently until the sugar has dissolved. Stir in the creamed coconut and chilli powder. When melted, remove from the heat and stir in the soy sauce and the peanut butter. Leave to cool slightly, then spoon into a serving dish.

Thread 3 prawns on to each of four skewers and divide the sliced beef between the remaining skewers. Cook the skewers under the preheated grill for 4–5 minutes, turning occasionally. The prawns should be opaque and pink and the beef browned on the outside, but still pink in the centre. Transfer to warmed individual serving plates, garnish with a few fresh coriander leaves and serve immediately with the warm peanut sauce.

Vietnamese Beef & Rice Noodle Soup

Serves 4–6

For the beef stock:

900 g/2 lb meaty beef bones
1 large onion, peeled and quartered
2 carrots, peeled and cut into chunks
2 celery stalks, trimmed and sliced
1 leek, washed and sliced into chunks
2 garlic cloves, unpeeled and lightly crushed
3 whole star anise
1 tsp black peppercorns

For the soup:

175 g/6 oz dried rice stick noodles
4–6 spring onions, trimmed and diagonally sliced
1 red chilli, deseeded and diagonally sliced
1 small bunch fresh coriander
1 small bunch fresh mint
350 g/12 oz fillet steak, very thinly sliced
salt and freshly ground black pepper

Place all the ingredients for the beef stock into a large stock pot or saucepan and cover with cold water. Bring to the boil and skim off any scum that rises to the surface. Reduce the heat and simmer gently, partially covered, for 2–3 hours, skimming occasionally.

Strain into a large bowl and leave to cool, then skim off the fat. Chill in the refrigerator and when cold remove any fat from the surface. Pour 1.7 litres/3 pints of the stock into a large wok and reserve.

Cover the noodles with warm water and leave for 3 minutes, or until just softened. Drain, then cut into 10 cm/4 inch lengths.

Arrange the spring onions and chilli on a serving platter or large plate. Strip the leaves from the coriander and mint and arrange them in piles on the plate.

Bring the stock in the wok to the boil over a high heat. Add the noodles and simmer for about 2 minutes, or until tender. Add the beef strips and simmer for about 1 minute. Season to taste with salt and pepper.

Ladle the soup with the noodles and beef strips into individual soup bowls and serve immediately with the plate of condiments handed around separately.

Barbecue Pork Steamed Buns

Serves 12

For the buns:
175–200 g/6–7 oz plain flour
1 tbsp dried yeast
125 ml/4 fl oz milk
2 tbsp sunflower oil
1 tbsp sugar
1/2 tsp salt
spring onion tassels, to garnish
fresh green salad leaves,
to serve

For the filling:
2 tbsp vegetable oil
1 small red pepper, deseeded and
finely chopped
2 garlic cloves, peeled and
finely chopped
225 g/8 oz cooked pork,
finely chopped
50 g/2 oz light brown sugar
50 ml/2 fl oz tomato ketchup
1–2 tsp hot chilli powder, or to taste

Put 75 g/3 oz of the flour in a bowl and stir in the yeast. Heat the milk, oil, sugar and salt in a small saucepan until warm, stirring until the sugar has dissolved. Pour into the bowl and, with an electric mixer, beat on a low speed for 30 seconds, scraping down the sides of the bowl, until blended. Beat at high speed for 3 minutes, then with a wooden spoon, stir in as much of the remaining flour as possible, until a stiff dough forms. Shape into a ball, place in a lightly oiled bowl, cover with clingfilm and leave for 1 hour in a warm place, or until doubled in size.

To make the filling, heat a wok, add the oil and when hot add the pepper and garlic. Stir-fry for 4–5 minutes. Add the remaining ingredients and bring to the boil, stir-frying for 2–3 minutes until thick and syrupy. Cool and reserve.

Punch down the dough and turn onto a lightly floured surface. Divide into 12 pieces, shape into balls, cover and leave to rest for 5 minutes. Roll each ball to a 7.5 cm/ 3 inch circle and place a heaped tablespoon of filling in the centre. For each circle, dampen the edges, then bring them up and around the filling, pinching together to seal. Place seam-side down on nonstick baking parchment. Leave to rise for 10 minutes.

Bring a large wok half-filled with water to the boil, place the buns in a lightly oiled Chinese steamer, without touching each other. Cover and steam for 20–25 minutes. Remove and cool slightly. Garnish and serve.

Sticky Braised Spare Ribs

Serves 4

900 g/2 lb meaty pork spare ribs,
cut crossways into
7.5 cm/3 inch pieces
125 ml/4 fl oz apricot nectar or
orange juice
50 ml/2 fl oz dry white wine
3 tbsp black bean sauce
3 tbsp tomato ketchup
2 tbsp clear honey
3–4 spring onions,
trimmed and chopped
2 garlic cloves, peeled and crushed
grated zest of 1 small orange
salt and freshly ground
black pepper

To garnish:

spring onion tassels
lemon wedges

Put the spare ribs in the wok and add enough cold water to cover. Bring to the boil over a medium-high heat, skimming any scum that rises to the surface. Cover and simmer for 30 minutes, then drain and rinse the ribs.

Rinse and dry the wok and return the ribs to it. In a bowl, blend the apricot nectar or orange juice with the white wine, black bean sauce, tomato ketchup and the honey until smooth.

Stir in the spring onions, garlic cloves and grated orange zest. Stir well until mixed thoroughly.

Pour the mixture over the spare ribs in the wok and stir gently until the ribs are lightly coated. Place over a moderate heat and bring to the boil.

Cover then simmer, stirring occasionally, for 1 hour, or until the ribs are tender and the sauce is thickened and sticky. (If the sauce reduces too quickly or begins to stick, add water 1 tablespoon at a time until the ribs are tender.) Adjust the seasoning to taste, then transfer the ribs to a serving plate and garnish with spring onion tassels and lemon wedges. Serve immediately.

Laksa Malayan Rice Noodle Soup

Serves 4–6

1.1 kg/2^1/$_2$ lb corn-fed,
free-range chicken
1 tsp black peppercorns
1 tbsp vegetable oil
1 large onion, peeled and thinly sliced
2 garlic cloves, peeled and
finely chopped
2.5 cm/1 inch piece fresh root ginger,
peeled and thinly sliced
1 tsp ground coriander
2 red chillies, deseeded and
diagonally sliced
1–2 tsp hot curry paste
400 ml/14 fl oz coconut milk
450 g/1 lb large raw prawns,
peeled and deveined
^{1}/$_2$ small head of Chinese leaves,
thinly shredded
1 tsp sugar
2 spring onions, trimmed and sliced
125 g/4 oz beansprouts
250 g/9 oz rice noodles or rice sticks,
soaked as per packet instructions
fresh mint leaves, to garnish

Put the chicken in a large saucepan with the peppercorns and cover with cold water. Bring to the boil, skimming off any scum that rises to the surface. Simmer, partially covered, for about 1 hour. Remove the chicken and cool. Skim any fat from the stock and strain through a muslin-lined sieve and reserve. Remove the meat from the carcass, shred and reserve.

Heat a large wok, add the oil and when hot, add the onions and stir-fry for 2 minutes, or until they begin to colour. Stir in the garlic, ginger, coriander, chillies and curry paste and stir-fry for a further 2 minutes.

Carefully pour in the reserved stock (you need at least 1.1 litres/ 2 pints) and simmer gently, partially covered, for 10 minutes, or until slightly reduced.

Add the coconut milk, prawns, Chinese leaves, sugar, spring onions and beansprouts and simmer for 3 minutes, stirring occasionally. Add the reserved shredded chicken, and cook for a further 2 minutes.

Drain the noodles and divide between 4–6 soup bowls. Ladle the hot stock and vegetables over the noodles, making sure each serving has some prawns and chicken. Garnish each bowl with fresh mint leaves and serve immediately.

Spring Rolls with Mixed Vegetables

Serves 12

2 tbsp sesame oil
125 g/4 oz broccoli florets, cut into small pieces
125 g/4 oz carrots, peeled and cut into matchsticks
125 g/4 oz courgettes, cut into strips
150 g/5 oz button mushrooms, finely chopped
2.5 cm/1 inch piece fresh root ginger, peeled and grated
1 garlic clove, peeled and finely chopped
4 spring onions, trimmed and finely chopped
75 g/3 oz beansprouts
1 tbsp light soy sauce
pinch cayenne pepper
4 tbsp plain flour
12 sheets filo pastry
300 ml/½ pint groundnut oil
spring onion curls, to garnish

Heat a wok, add the sesame oil and when hot, add the chopped broccoli, carrots, courgettes, mushrooms, ginger, garlic and spring onions and stir-fry for 1–2 minutes, or until slightly softened.

Turn into a bowl, add the beansprouts, soy sauce and cayenne pepper and mix together. Transfer the vegetables to a colander and drain for 5 minutes. Meanwhile, blend the flour with 2–3 tablespoons of water to form a paste and reserve.

Fold a sheet of filo pastry in half and in half again, brushing a little water between each layer. Place a spoonful of the drained vegetable mixture on the pastry. Brush a little of the flour paste along the edges. Turn the edges into the centre, then roll up and seal. Repeat with the rest.

Wipe the wok clean, return to the heat, add the oil and heat to 190°C/375°F. Add the spring rolls in batches and deep-fry for 2–3 minutes, or until golden. Drain on absorbent kitchen paper, arrange on a platter, garnish with spring onion curls and serve immediately.

Moo Shi Pork

Serves 4

175 g/6 oz pork fillet
2 tsp Chinese rice wine or dry sherry
2 tbsp light soy sauce
1 tsp cornflour
25 g/1 oz dried golden needles,
soaked and drained
2 tbsp groundnut oil
3 medium eggs, lightly beaten
1 tsp freshly grated root ginger
3 spring onions, trimmed and
thinly sliced
150 g/5 oz bamboo shoots, cut into
fine strips
salt and freshly ground black pepper
8 mandarin pancakes, steamed
hoisin sauce
sprigs of fresh coriander, to garnish

Cut the pork across the grain into 1 cm/½ inch slices, then cut into thin strips. Place in a bowl with the Chinese rice wine or sherry, soy sauce and cornflour. Mix well and reserve. Trim off the tough ends of the golden needles, then cut in half and reserve.

Heat a wok or large frying pan, add 1 tablespoon of the groundnut oil and when hot, add the lightly beaten eggs, and cook for 1 minute, stirring all the time, until scrambled. Remove and reserve. Wipe the wok clean with absorbent kitchen paper.

Return the wok to the heat, add the remaining oil and when hot transfer the pork strips from the marinade mixture to the wok, shaking off as much marinade as possible. Stir-fry for 30 seconds, then add the ginger, spring onions and bamboo shoots and pour in the marinade. Stir-fry for 2–3 minutes or until cooked.

Return the scrambled eggs to the wok, season to taste with salt and ground black pepper and stir for a few seconds until mixed well and heated through. Divide the mixture between the pancakes, drizzle each with 1 teaspoon of hoisin sauce and roll up. Garnish and serve immediately.

Spicy Prawns in Lettuce Cups

Serves 4

1 lemon grass stalk

225 g/8 oz peeled cooked prawns

1 tsp finely grated lime zest

1 red bird's-eye chilli, deseeded and finely chopped

2.5 cm/1 inch piece fresh root ginger, peeled and grated

2 Little Gem lettuces, divided into leaves

25 g/1 oz roasted peanuts, chopped

2 spring onions, trimmed and diagonally sliced

sprig fresh coriander, to garnish

For the coconut sauce:

2 tbsp freshly grated or unsweetened shredded coconut

1 tbsp hoisin sauce

1 tbsp light soy sauce

1 tbsp Thai fish sauce

1 tbsp palm sugar or soft light brown sugar

Remove three or four of the tougher outer leaves of the lemon grass and reserve for another dish. Finely chop the remaining softer centre. Place 2 teaspoons of the chopped lemon grass in a bowl with the prawns, grated lime zest, chilli and ginger. Mix together to coat the prawns. Cover and place in the refrigerator to marinate while you make the coconut sauce.

For the sauce, place the grated coconut in a wok or nonstick frying pan and dry-fry for 2–3 minutes or until golden. Remove from the pan and reserve. Add the hoisin, soy and fish sauces to the pan with the sugar and 4 tablespoons of water. Simmer for 2–3 minutes, then remove from the heat. Leave to cool.

Pour the sauce over the prawns, add the toasted coconut and toss to mix together. Divide the prawn and coconut sauce mixture between the lettuce leaves and arrange on a platter.

Sprinkle over the chopped roasted peanuts and spring onions and garnish with a sprig of fresh coriander. Serve immediately.

Crispy Pork Wontons

Serves 4

1 small onion, peeled and
roughly chopped
2 garlic cloves, peeled and crushed
1 green chilli, deseeded
and chopped
2.5 cm/1 inch piece fresh root
ginger, peeled and
roughly chopped
450 g/1 lb lean pork mince
4 tbsp freshly chopped coriander
1 tsp Chinese five-spice powder
salt and freshly ground
black pepper
20 wonton wrappers
1 medium egg, lightly beaten
vegetable oil for deep-frying
chilli sauce, to serve

Place the onion, garlic, chilli and ginger in a food processor and blend until very finely chopped. Add the pork, coriander and Chinese five-spice powder. Season the mixture to taste with salt and pepper, then blend again briefly to mix. Divide the mixture into 20 equal portions and with floured hands shape each into a walnut-sized ball.

Brush the edges of a wonton wrapper with beaten egg, place a pork ball in the centre, then bring the corners to the centre and pinch together to make a money bag. Repeat with the remaining pork balls and wrappers.

Pour sufficient oil into a heavy-based saucepan or deep-fat fryer so that it is one-third full and heat to 180˚C/ 350˚F. Deep-fry the wontons in three or four batches for 3–4 minutes, or until cooked through and golden and crisp. Drain on absorbent kitchen paper. Serve the crispy pork wontons immediately, allowing five per person, with some chilli sauce for dipping.

Sesame Prawn Toasts

Serves 4

125 g/4 oz peeled cooked prawns
1 tbsp cornflour
2 spring onions, peeled and
roughly chopped
2 tsp freshly grated root ginger
2 tsp dark soy sauce
pinch Chinese five-spice powder
(optional)
1 small egg, beaten
salt and freshly ground black pepper
6 thin slices day-old white bread
40 g/1 1/2 oz sesame seeds
vegetable oil for deep-frying
chilli sauce, to serve

Place the prawns in a food processor or blender with the cornflour, spring onions, ginger, soy sauce and Chinese five spice powder, if using. Blend to a fairly smooth paste. Spoon into a bowl and stir in the beaten egg. Season to taste with salt and pepper.

Cut the crusts off the bread. Spread the prawn paste in an even layer on one side of each slice. Sprinkle over the sesame seeds and press down lightly.

Cut each slice diagonally into four triangles. Place on a board and chill in the refrigerator for 30 minutes.

Pour sufficient oil into a heavy-based saucepan or deep-fat fryer so that it is one-third full. Heat until it reaches a temperature of 180°C/350°F. Cook the toasts in batches of five or six, carefully lowering them seeded-side down into the oil. Deep-fry for 2–3 minutes, or until lightly browned, then turn over and cook for 1 minute more. Using a slotted spoon, lift out the toasts and drain on absorbent kitchen paper. Keep warm while frying the remaining toasts. Arrange on a warmed platter and serve immediately with some chilli sauce for dipping.

Spicy Beef Pancakes

Serves 4

50 g/2 oz plain flour
pinch salt
$^1/_2$ tsp Chinese five-spice powder
1 large egg yolk
150 ml/$^1/_4$ pint milk
4 tsp sunflower oil
slices of spring onion, to garnish

For the spicy beef filling:

1 tbsp sesame oil
4 spring onions, sliced
1 cm/$^1/_2$ inch piece fresh root ginger,
peeled and grated
1 garlic clove, peeled and crushed
300 g/11 oz sirloin steak, trimmed
and cut into strips
1 red chilli, deseeded and
finely chopped
1 tsp sherry vinegar
1 tsp soft dark brown sugar
1 tbsp dark soy sauce

Sift the flour, salt and Chinese five-spice powder into a bowl and make a well in the centre. Add the egg yolk and a little of the milk. Gradually beat in, drawing in the flour to make a smooth batter. Whisk in the rest of the milk.

Heat 1 teaspoon of the sunflower oil in a small heavy-based frying pan. Pour in just enough batter to thinly coat the base of the pan. Cook over a medium heat for 1 minute, or until the underside of the pancake is golden brown.

Turn or toss the pancake and cook for 1 minute, or until the other side of the pancake is golden brown. Make seven more pancakes with the remaining batter. Stack them on a warmed plate as you make them, with greaseproof paper between each pancake. Cover with kitchen foil and keep warm in a low oven.

Make the filling. Heat a wok or large frying pan, add the sesame oil and when hot, add the spring onions, ginger and garlic and stir-fry for 1 minute. Add the beef strips, stir-fry for 3–4 minutes, then stir in the chilli, vinegar, sugar and soy sauce. Cook for 1 minute, then remove from the heat.

Spoon one eighth of the filling over one half of each pancake. Fold the pancakes in half, then fold in half again. Garnish with a few slices of spring onion and serve immediately.

Thai Shellfish Soup

Serves 4–6

350 g/12 oz raw prawns
350 g/12 oz firm white fish, such as
monkfish, cod or haddock
175 g/ 6 oz small squid rings
1 tbsp lime juice
450 g/1 lb live mussels
400 ml/15 fl oz coconut milk
1 tbsp groundnut oil
2 tbsp Thai red curry paste
1 lemon grass stalk, bruised
3 kaffir lime leaves, finely shredded
2 tbsp Thai fish sauce
salt and freshly ground
black pepper
fresh coriander leaves, to garnish

Peel the prawns. Using a sharp knife, remove the black vein along the back of the prawns. Pat dry with absorbent kitchen paper and reserve.

Skin the fish, pat dry and cut into 2.5 cm/1 inch chunks. Place in a bowl with the prawns and the squid rings. Sprinkle with the lime juice and reserve.

Scrub the mussels, removing their beards and any barnacles. Discard any mussels that are open, damaged or that do not close when tapped. Place in a large saucepan and add 150 ml/¼ pint of the coconut milk.

Cover, bring to the boil, then simmer for 5 minutes, or until the mussels open, shaking the saucepan occasionally. Lift out the mussels, discarding any unopened ones, strain the liquid through a muslin-lined sieve and reserve.

Rinse and dry the saucepan. Heat the groundnut oil, add the curry paste and cook for 1 minute, stirring all the time. Add the lemon grass, lime leaves, fish sauce and pour in both the strained and the remaining coconut milk. Bring the contents of the saucepan to a very gentle simmer.

Add the fish mixture to the saucepan and simmer for 2–3 minutes or until just cooked. Stir in the mussels, with or without their shells as preferred. Season to taste with salt and pepper, then garnish with coriander leaves. Ladle into warmed bowls and serve immediately.

Cantonese Chicken Wings

Serves 4

3 tbsp hoisin sauce

2 tbsp dark soy sauce

1 tbsp sesame oil

1 garlic clove, peeled and crushed

2.5 cm/1 inch piece fresh root ginger, peeled and grated

1 tbsp Chinese rice wine or dry sherry

2 tsp chilli bean sauce

2 tsp red or white wine vinegar

2 tbsp soft light brown sugar

900 g/2 lb large chicken wings

50 g/2 oz cashew nuts, chopped

2 spring onions, trimmed and finely chopped

Preheat the oven to 220°C/ 425°F/Gas Mark 7, 15 minutes before cooking. Place the hoisin sauce, soy sauce, sesame oil, garlic, ginger, Chinese rice wine or sherry, chilli bean sauce, vinegar and sugar in a small saucepan with 6 tablespoons of water. Bring to the boil, stirring occasionally, then simmer for about 30 seconds. Remove the glaze from the heat.

Place the chicken wings in a roasting tin in a single layer. Pour over the glaze and stir until the wings are coated thoroughly.

Cover the tin loosely with kitchen foil, place in the preheated oven and roast for 25 minutes. Remove the kitchen foil, baste the wings and cook for a further 5 minutes.

Reduce the oven temperature to 190°C/375°F/Gas Mark 5. Turn the wings over and sprinkle with the chopped cashew nuts and spring onions. Return to the oven and cook for 5 minutes, or until the nuts are lightly browned, the glaze is sticky and the wings are tender. Remove from the oven and leave to stand for 5 minutes before arranging on a warmed platter. Serve immediately with finger bowls and plenty of napkins.

Crispy Prawns with Chinese Dipping Sauce

Serves 4

450 g/1 lb medium-sized raw
prawns, peeled
¼ tsp salt
6 tbsp groundnut oil
2 garlic cloves, peeled and
finely chopped
2.5 cm/1 inch piece fresh root
ginger, peeled and finely chopped
1 green chilli, deseeded and
finely chopped
4 stems fresh coriander, leaves
and stems roughly chopped

For the Chinese dipping sauce:

3 tbsp dark soy sauce
3 tbsp rice wine vinegar
1 tbsp caster sugar
2 tbsp chilli oil
2 spring onions, finely shredded

Using a sharp knife, remove the black vein along the back of the prawns. Sprinkle the prawns with the salt and leave to stand for 15 minutes. Pat dry on absorbent kitchen paper.

Heat a wok or large frying pan, add the groundnut oil and when hot, add the prawns and stir-fry in two batches for about 1 minute, or until they turn pink and are almost cooked. Using a slotted spoon, remove the prawns and keep warm in a low oven.

Drain the oil from the wok, leaving 1 tablespoon. Add the garlic, ginger and chilli and cook for about 30 seconds. Add the coriander, return the prawns and stir-fry for 1–2 minutes, or until the prawns are cooked through and the garlic is golden. Turn into a warmed serving dish.

For the dipping sauce, using a fork, beat together the soy sauce, rice vinegar, caster sugar and chilli oil in a small bowl. Stir in the spring onions. Serve immediately with the hot prawns.

Vegetable Thai Spring Rolls

Serves 4

50 g/2 oz cellophane vermicelli
4 dried shiitake mushrooms
1 tbsp groundnut oil
2 medium carrots, peeled and cut
into fine matchsticks
125 g/4 oz mangetout, cut
lengthways into fine strips
3 spring onions, trimmed
and chopped
125 g/4 oz canned bamboo shoots,
cut into fine matchsticks
1 cm/½ inch piece fresh root ginger,
peeled and grated
1 tbsp light soy sauce
1 medium egg, separated
salt and freshly ground
black pepper
20 spring roll wrappers, each about
12.5 cm/5 inch square
vegetable oil for deep-frying
spring onion tassels, to garnish

Place the vermicelli in a bowl and pour over enough boiling water to cover. Leave to soak for 5 minutes or until softened, then drain. Cut into 7.5 cm/3 inch lengths. Soak the shiitake mushrooms in almost boiling water for 15 minutes, drain, discard the stalks and slice thinly.

Heat a wok or large frying pan, add the groundnut oil and when hot, add the carrots and stir-fry for 1 minute. Add the mangetout and spring onions and stir-fry for 2–3 minutes or until tender. Tip the vegetables into a bowl and leave to cool. Stir the vermicelli and shiitake mushrooms into the cooled vegetables with the bamboo shoots, ginger, soy sauce and egg yolk. Season to taste with salt and pepper and mix thoroughly.

Brush the edges of a spring roll wrapper with a little beaten egg white. Spoon 2 teaspoons of the vegetable filling on to the wrapper, in a 7.5 cm/3 inch log shape 2.5 cm/1 inch from one edge. Fold the wrapper edge over the filling, then fold in the right and left sides. Brush the folded edges with more egg white and roll up neatly. Place on an oiled baking sheet, seam-side down and make the rest of the spring rolls.

5 Heat the oil in a heavy-based saucepan or deep-fat fryer to 180°C/350°F. Deep-fry the spring rolls, six at a time for 2–3 minutes, or until golden brown and crisp. Drain on absorbent kitchen paper and arrange on a warmed platter. Garnish with spring onion tassels and serve immediately.

Sesame Prawns

Serves 6–8

24 large raw prawns
40 g/1 oz plain flour
4 tbsp sesame seeds
salt and freshly ground black pepper
1 large egg
300 ml/¹/₂ pint vegetable oil
for deep frying

For the soy dipping sauce:

50 ml/2 fl oz soy sauce
1 spring onion, trimmed and
finely chopped
¹/₂ tsp dried crushed chillies
1 tbsp sesame oil
1–2 tsp sugar, or to taste
strips of spring onion, to garnish

Remove the heads from the prawns by twisting away from the body and discard. Peel the prawns, leaving the tails on for presentation. With a sharp knife, remove the black vein from the back of the prawns. Rinse and dry.

Slice along the back, but do not cut through the prawn body. Place on the chopping board and press to flatten slightly, to make a butterfly shape.

Put the flour, half the sesame seeds, salt and pepper into a food processor and blend for 30 seconds. Tip into a polythene bag and add the prawns, 4–5 at a time. Twist to seal, then shake to coat with the flour.

Beat the egg in bowl with the remaining sesame seeds, salt and pepper.

Heat the oil in a large wok to 190˚C/ 375˚F, or until a small cube of bread browns in about 30 seconds. Working in batches of five or six, and holding each prawn by the tail, dip into the beaten egg, then carefully lower into the oil. Cook for 1–2 minutes, or until crisp and golden, turning once or twice. Using a slotted spoon, remove the prawns, drain on absorbent kitchen paper and keep warm.

To make the dipping sauce, stir together the soy sauce, spring onion, chillies, oil and sugar until the sugar dissolves. Arrange the prawns on a plate, garnish with strips of spring onion and serve immediately.

Chicken-filled Spring Rolls

Makes 12–14 rolls

For the filling:
1 tbsp vegetable oil
2 slices streaky bacon, diced
225 g/8 oz skinless chicken
breast fillets, thinly sliced
1 small red pepper,
deseeded and finely chopped
4 spring onions, trimmed and chopped
2.5 cm/1 inch piece fresh root
ginger, peeled and finely chopped
75 g/3 oz mangetout peas, thinly sliced
75 g/3 oz beansprouts
1 tbsp soy sauce
2 tsp Chinese rice wine or dry sherry
2 tsp hoisin or plum sauce

For the wrappers:
3 tbsp plain flour
12–14 spring roll wrappers
300 ml/½ pint vegetable oil for
deep frying
shredded spring onions, to garnish
dipping sauce, to serve

Heat a large wok, add the oil and when hot add the diced bacon and stir-fry for 2–3 minutes, or until golden. Add the chicken and pepper and stir-fry for a further 2–3 minutes. Add the remaining filling ingredients and stir-fry 3–4 minutes until all the vegetables are tender. Turn into a colander and leave to drain as the mixture cools completely.

Blend the flour with about 1½ tablespoons of water to form a paste. Soften each wrapper in a plate of warm water for 1–2 seconds, then place on a chopping board. Put 2–3 tablespoons of filling on the near edge. Fold the edge over the filling to cover. Fold in each side and roll up. Seal the edge with a little flour paste and press to seal securely. Transfer to a baking sheet, seam-side down.

Heat the oil in a large wok to 190°C/375°F, or until a small cube of bread browns in about 30 seconds. Working in batches of three to four, fry the spring rolls until they are crisp and golden, turning once (about 2 minutes). Remove and drain on absorbent kitchen paper. Arrange the spring rolls on a serving plate, garnish with spring onion tassels and serve hot with dipping sauce.

Soy-glazed Chicken Thighs

Serves 6–8

900 g/2 lb chicken thighs
2 tbsp vegetable oil
3–4 garlic cloves, peeled
and crushed
4 cm/1¹/₂ inch piece fresh root
ginger, peeled and finely
chopped or grated
125 ml/4 fl oz soy sauce
2–3 tbsp Chinese rice wine or
dry sherry
2 tbsp clear honey
1 tbsp soft brown sugar
2–3 dashes hot chilli sauce,
or to taste
freshly chopped parsley, to garnish

Heat a large wok and when hot add the oil and heat. Stir-fry the chicken thighs for 5 minutes or until golden. Remove and drain on absorbent kitchen paper. You may need to do this in two to three batches.

Pour off the oil and fat and, using absorbent kitchen paper, carefully wipe out the wok. Add the garlic, with the root ginger, soy sauce, Chinese rice wine or sherry and honey to the wok and stir well. Sprinkle in the soft brown sugar with the hot chilli sauce to taste, then place over the heat and bring to the boil.

Reduce the heat to a gentle simmer, then carefully add the chicken thighs. Cover the wok and simmer gently over a very low heat for 30 minutes, or until they are tender and the sauce is reduced and thickened and glazes the chicken thighs.

Stir or spoon the sauce occasionally over the chicken thighs and add a little water if the sauce is starting to become too thick. Arrange in a shallow serving dish, garnish with freshly chopped parsley and serve immediately.

Shredded Duck in Lettuce Leaves

Serves 4–6

15 g/¹/₂ oz dried Chinese (shiitake)
mushrooms
2 tbsp vegetable oil
400 g/14 oz boneless, skinless
duck breast, cut crossways into
thin strips
1 red chilli, deseeded and
diagonally thinly sliced
4–6 spring onions, trimmed and
diagonally sliced
2 garlic cloves, peeled and crushed
75 g/3 oz beansprouts
3 tbsp soy sauce
1 tbsp Chinese rice wine or
dry sherry
1–2 tsp clear honey or
brown sugar
4–6 tbsp hoisin sauce
large, crisp lettuce leaves such as
iceberg or cos
handful fresh mint leaves
dipping sauce (see Sesame
Prawns, page 56)

Cover the dried Chinese mushrooms with almost boiling water, leave for 20 minutes, then drain and slice thinly.

Heat a large wok, add the oil and when hot stir-fry the duck for 3–4 minutes, or until sealed. Remove with a slotted spoon and reserve.

Add the chilli, spring onions, garlic and Chinese mushrooms to the wok and stir-fry for 2–3 minutes, or until softened.

Add the beansprouts, the soy sauce, Chinese rice wine or dry sherry and honey or brown sugar to the wok, and continue to stir-fry for 1 minute, or until blended.

Stir in the reserved duck and stir-fry for 2 minutes, or until well mixed together and heated right through. Transfer to a heated serving dish.

Arrange the hoisin sauce in a small bowl on a tray or plate with a pile of lettuce leaves and the mint leaves.

Let each guest spoon a little hoisin sauce onto a lettuce leaf, then top with a large spoonful of the stir-fried duck and vegetables and roll up the leaf to enclose the filling. Serve with the dipping sauce.

Thai Crab Cakes

Serves 4

200 g/7 oz easy-cook basmati rice
450 ml/³/₄ pint chicken stock, heated
200 g/7 oz cooked crab meat
125 g/4 oz cod fillet, skinned
and minced
5 spring onions, trimmed and
finely chopped
1 lemon grass stalk, outer leaves
discarded and finely chopped
1 green chilli, deseeded and
finely chopped
1 tbsp freshly grated root ginger
1 tbsp freshly chopped coriander
1 tbsp plain flour
1 medium egg
salt and freshly ground black pepper
2 tbsp vegetable oil, for frying

To serve:

sweet chilli dipping sauce
fresh salad leaves

Put the rice in a large saucepan and add the hot stock. Bring to the boil, cover and simmer over a low heat, without stirring, for 18 minutes, or until the grains are tender and all the liquid is absorbed.

To make the cakes, place the crab meat, fish, spring onions, lemon grass, chilli, ginger, coriander, flour and egg in a food processor. Blend until all the ingredients are mixed thoroughly, then season to taste with salt and pepper. Add the rice to the processor and blend once more, but do not over mix.

Remove the mixture from the processor and place on a clean work surface. With damp hands, divide into 12 even-sized patties. Transfer to a plate, cover and chill in the refrigerator for about 30 minutes.

Heat the oil in a heavy-based frying pan and cook the crab cakes, 4 at a time, for 3–5 minutes on each side until crisp and golden. Drain on absorbent kitchen paper and serve immediately with a chilli dipping sauce.

Wonton Noodle Soup

Serves 4

4 shiitake mushrooms, wiped
125 g/4 oz raw prawns, peeled and
finely chopped
125 g/4 oz pork mince
4 water chestnuts, finely chopped
4 spring onions, trimmed and
finely sliced
1 medium egg white
salt and freshly ground black pepper
1¹/₂ tsp cornflour
1 packet fresh wonton wrappers
1.1 litres/2 pints chicken stock
2 cm/³/₄ inch piece root ginger,
peeled and sliced
75 g/3 oz thin egg noodles
125 g/4 oz pak choi, shredded

Place the mushrooms in a bowl, cover with warm water and leave to soak for 1 hour. Drain, remove and discard the stalks and finely chop the mushrooms. Return to the bowl with the prawns, pork, water chestnuts, 2 of the spring onions and egg white. Season to taste with salt and pepper. Mix well.

Mix the cornflour with 1 tablespoon of cold water to make a paste. Place a wonton wrapper on a board and brush the edges with the paste. Drop a little less than 1 teaspoon of the pork mixture in the centre then fold in half to make a triangle, pressing the edges together. Bring the two outer corners together, fixing together with a little more paste. Continue until all the pork mixture is used up; you should have 16–20 wontons.

Pour the stock into a large wide saucepan, add the ginger slices and bring to the boil. Add the wontons and simmer for about 5 minutes. Add the noodles and cook for 1 minute. Stir in the pak choi and cook for a further 2 minutes, or until the noodles and pak choi are tender and the wontons have floated to the surface and are cooked through.

Ladle the soup into warmed bowls, discarding the ginger. Sprinkle with the remaining sliced spring onion and serve immediately.

Chinese Leaf Mushroom Soup

Serves 4–6

450 g/1 lb Chinese leaves
25 g/1 oz dried Chinese (shiitake) mushrooms
1 tbsp vegetable oil
75 g/3 oz smoked streaky bacon, diced
2.5 cm/1 inch piece fresh root ginger, peeled and finely chopped
175 g/6 oz chestnut mushrooms, thinly sliced
1.1 litres/2 pints chicken stock
4–6 spring onions, trimmed and cut into short lengths
2 tbsp dry sherry or Chinese rice wine
salt and freshly ground black pepper
sesame oil for drizzling

Trim the stem ends of the Chinese leaves and cut in half lengthways. Remove the triangular core with a knife, then cut into 2.5 cm/1 inch slices and reserve.

Place the dried Chinese mushrooms in a bowl and pour over enough almost boiling water to cover. Leave to stand for 20 minutes to soften, then gently lift out and squeeze out the liquid. Discard the stems and thinly slice the caps and reserve. Strain the liquid through a muslin-lined sieve or a coffee filter paper and reserve.

Heat a wok over a medium-high heat, add the oil and when hot add the bacon. Stir-fry for 3–4 minutes, or until crisp and golden, stirring frequently. Add the ginger and chestnut mushrooms and stir-fry for a further 2–3 minutes.

Add the chicken stock and bring to the boil, skimming any fat and scum that rises to the surface. Add the spring onions, sherry or rice wine, Chinese leaves, sliced Chinese mushrooms and season to taste with salt and pepper. Pour in the reserved soaking liquid and reduce the heat to the lowest possible setting. Simmer gently, covered, until all the vegetables are very tender; this will take about 10 minutes. Add a little water if the liquid has reduced too much. Spoon into soup bowls and drizzle with a little sesame oil. Serve immediately.

Meat

South-East Asian meat dishes are as varied as they are delicious. Featuring a wide selection of dishes containing pork, beef, lamb and more, the mouthwatering recipes in this chapter will inspire you to extend your cooking repertoire. From Vietnamese-style Braised Pork to Malaysian Beef Satay, the wealth of fresh ingredients and spice combinations guarantee that there is a recipe for every mood and occasion.

Nasi Goreng

Serves 4

7 large shallots, peeled
1 red chilli, deseeded and
roughly chopped
2 garlic cloves, peeled and
roughly chopped
4 tbsp sunflower oil
2 tsp each tomato purée and
Indonesian sweet soy sauce
(ketjap manis)
225 g/8 oz long-grain white rice
125 g/4 oz French beans, trimmed
3 medium eggs, beaten
pinch sugar
salt and freshly ground black pepper
225 g/8 oz cooked ham, shredded
225 g/8 oz cooked peeled prawns,
thawed if frozen
6 spring onions, trimmed and
thinly sliced
1 tbsp light soy sauce
3 tbsp freshly chopped coriander

Roughly chop 1 of the shallots and place with the red chilli, garlic, 1 tablespoon of the oil, tomato purée and sweet soy sauce in a food processor. Blend until smooth, then reserve. Boil the rice for 6–7 minutes until tender, adding the French beans after 4 minutes. Drain and cool.

Beat the eggs with the sugar and a little salt and pepper. Heat a little of the oil in a small nonstick frying pan and add about one third of the egg mixture. Swirl to coat the base of the pan thinly and cook for about 1 minute until golden. Flip and cook the other side briefly before removing from the pan. Roll the omelette and slice thinly into strips. Repeat with the remaining egg to make 3 omelettes.

Heat 2 tablespoons of the oil in a clean frying pan. Thinly slice the remaining shallots, add to the pan and cook for 8–10 minutes over a medium heat until golden and crisp. Drain on absorbent kitchen paper and reserve.

Add the remaining 1 tablespoon of oil to a large wok or frying pan and fry the chilli paste over a medium heat for 1 minute. Add the cooked rice and beans and stir-fry for 2 minutes. Add the ham and prawns and continue stir-frying for a further 1–2 minutes. Add the omelette slices, half the fried shallots, the spring onions, soy sauce and chopped coriander. Stir-fry for a further minute until heated through. Spoon onto serving plates and garnish with the remaining crispy shallots. Serve immediately.

Chinese Bean Sauce Noodles

Serves 4

250 g/9 oz fine egg noodles
1¹/₂ tbsp sesame oil
1 tbsp groundnut oil
3 garlic cloves, peeled and
finely chopped
4 spring onions, trimmed and
finely chopped
450 g/1 lb fresh pork mince
100 ml/4 fl oz crushed yellow
bean sauce
1–2 tsp hot chilli sauce
1 tbsp Chinese rice wine or
dry sherry
2 tbsp dark soy sauce
¹/₂ tsp cayenne pepper
2 tsp sugar
150 ml/¹/₄ pint chicken stock

Put the noodles into a large bowl and pour over boiling water to cover. Leave to soak according to packet instructions until tender. Drain well and place in a bowl with the sesame oil. Toss together well and reserve.

Heat a wok until it is hot, add the groundnut oil and when it is hot, add the garlic and half the spring onions. Stir-fry for a few seconds, then add the pork. Stir well to break up and continue to stir-fry for 1–2 minutes until it changes colour.

Add the yellow bean sauce, chilli sauce, Chinese rice wine or sherry, soy sauce, cayenne pepper, sugar and chicken stock, stirring all the time. Bring to the boil, reduce the heat and simmer for 5 minutes.

Meanwhile, bring a large saucepan of water to the boil and add the noodles for about 20 seconds. Drain well and tip into a warmed serving bowl. Pour the sauce over the top, sprinkle with the remaining spring onions and mix well. Serve immediately.

Spicy Pork

Serves 4

4 tbsp groundnut oil
2.5 cm/1 inch piece fresh root ginger, peeled and cut into matchsticks
1 garlic clove, peeled and chopped
2 medium carrots, peeled and cut into matchsticks
1 medium aubergine, trimmed and cubed
700 g/1½ lb pork fillet, thickly sliced
400 ml/14 fl oz coconut milk
2 tbsp Thai red curry paste
4 tbsp Thai fish sauce
2 tsp caster sugar
227 g can bamboo shoots in brine, drained and cut into matchsticks
salt, to taste
lime zest, to garnish
freshly cooked rice, to serve

Heat a wok or large frying pan, add 2 tablespoons of the oil and when hot, add the chopped ginger, garlic, carrots and aubergine and stir-fry for 3 minutes. Using a slotted spoon, transfer to a plate and keep warm.

Add the remaining oil to the wok, heat until smoking, then add the pork and stir-fry for 5–8 minutes or until browned all over. Transfer to a plate and keep warm. Wipe the wok clean.

Pour half the coconut milk into the wok, stir in the red curry paste and bring to the boil. Boil rapidly for 4 minutes, stirring occasionally, or until the sauce is reduced by half.

Add the fish sauce and sugar to the wok and bring back to the boil. Return the pork and vegetables to the wok with the bamboo shoots. Return to the boil, then simmer for 4 minutes.

Stir in the remaining coconut milk and season to taste with salt. Simmer for 2 minutes or until heated through. Garnish with lime zest and serve immediately with rice.

Pork with Tofu & Coconut

Serves 4

50 g/2 oz unsalted cashew nuts
1 tbsp ground coriander
1 tbsp ground cumin
2 tsp hot chilli powder
2.5 cm/1 inch piece fresh root ginger, peeled and chopped
1 tbsp oyster sauce
4 tbsp groundnut oil
400 ml/14 fl oz coconut milk
175 g/6 oz rice noodles
450 g/1 lb pork tenderloin, thickly sliced
1 red chilli, deseeded and sliced
1 green chilli, deseeded and sliced
1 bunch spring onions, trimmed and thickly sliced
3 tomatoes, roughly chopped
75 g/3 oz tofu, drained
2 tbsp freshly chopped coriander
2 tbsp freshly chopped mint
salt and freshly ground black pepper

Place the cashew nuts, coriander, cumin, chilli powder, ginger and oyster sauce in a food processor and blend until well ground. Heat a wok or large frying pan, add 2 tablespoons of the oil and when hot, add the cashew mixture and stir-fry for 1 minute. Stir in the coconut milk, bring to the boil, then simmer for 1 minute. Pour into a small jug and reserve. Wipe the wok clean.

Meanwhile, place the rice noodles in a bowl, cover with boiling water, leave to stand for 5 minutes, then drain thoroughly.

Reheat the wok, add the remaining oil and when hot, add the pork and stir-fry for 5 minutes or until browned all over. Add the chillies and spring onions and stir-fry for 2 minutes.

Add the tomatoes and tofu to the wok with the noodles and coconut mixture and stir-fry for a further 2 minutes, or until heated through, being careful not to break up the tofu. Sprinkle with the chopped coriander and mint, season to taste with salt and pepper and stir. Tip into a warmed serving dish and serve immediately.

Sweet-&-Sour Pork

Serves 4

450 g/1 lb pork fillet
1 medium egg white
4 tsp cornflour
salt and freshly ground
black pepper
300 ml/$\frac{1}{2}$ pint groundnut oil
1 small onion, peeled and
finely sliced
125 g/4 oz carrots, peeled and cut
into matchsticks
2.5 cm/1 inch piece fresh root
ginger, peeled and cut into
thin strips
150 ml/$\frac{1}{4}$ pint orange juice
150 ml/$\frac{1}{4}$ pint chicken stock
1 tbsp light soy sauce
220 g can pineapple pieces,
drained with juice reserved
1 tbsp white wine vinegar
1 tbsp freshly chopped parsley
freshly cooked rice, to serve

Trim, then cut the pork fillet into small cubes. In a bowl, whisk the egg white and cornflour with a little seasoning, then add the pork to the egg white mixture and stir until the cubes are well coated.

Heat the wok, then add the oil and heat until very hot before adding the pork and stir-frying for 30 seconds. Turn off the heat and continue to stir for 3 minutes. The meat should be white and sealed. Drain off and reserve 2 teaspoons of the oil, reserve the pork and wipe the wok clean.

Pour the reserved groundnut oil back into the wok and cook the onion, carrots and ginger for 2–3 minutes. Blend the orange juice with the chicken stock and soy sauce and make up to 300 ml/$\frac{1}{2}$ pint with the reserved pineapple juice.

Return the pork to the wok with the juice mixture and simmer for 3–4 minutes. Then stir in the pineapple pieces and vinegar. Heat through, then sprinkle with the chopped parsley and serve immediately with freshly cooked rice.

Vietnamese-style Braised Pork

Serves 4–6

550 g/1¼ lb pork tenderloin
2 tbsp vegetable oil
6 spring onions, trimmed and halved
5 cm/2 inch piece fresh root
ginger, chopped
2 lemon grass stalks, bruised,
outer leaves discarded
2–4 bird's eye chillies, deseeded
2 kaffir lime leaves
600 ml/1 pint chicken or
vegetable stock
1 tbsp clear honey
salt and freshly ground black pepper
1 tbsp fish sauce, or to taste
1 tbsp freshly chopped coriander

To serve:

freshly cooked fragrant rice
stir-fried vegetables

Trim the pork and cut into four portions. Heat the oil in a large saucepan or frying pan, add the pork and brown on all sides. Remove and reserve.

Place the reserved pork, spring onions, ginger, lemon grass, chillies and lime leaves in a clean saucepan and add the stock and honey. Bring to the boil, then reduce the heat and simmer gently for 30 minutes, or until tender.

Add salt and pepper to taste with the fish sauce, then serve the pork sprinkled with chopped coriander on a bed of rice with the stir-fried vegetables.

Pork Fried Noodles

Serves 4

125 g/4 oz dried thread egg noodles
125 g/4 oz broccoli florets
4 tbsp groundnut oil
350 g/12 oz pork tenderloin,
cut into slices
3 tbsp soy sauce
1 tbsp lemon juice
pinch sugar
1 tsp chilli sauce
1 tbsp sesame oil
2.5 cm/1 inch piece fresh root
ginger, peeled and cut into sticks
1 garlic clove, peeled and chopped
1 green chilli, deseeded and sliced
125 g/4 oz mangetout, halved
2 medium eggs, lightly beaten
227 g can water chestnuts, drained
and sliced

To garnish:

radish rose
spring onion tassels

Place the noodles in a bowl and cover with boiling water. Leave to stand for 20 minutes, stirring occasionally, or until tender. Drain and reserve. Meanwhile, blanch the broccoli in a saucepan of lightly salted boiling water for 2 minutes. Drain, refresh under cold running water and reserve.

Heat a large wok or frying pan, add the groundnut oil and heat until just smoking. Add the pork and stir-fry for 5 minutes, or until browned. Using a slotted spoon, remove the pork slices and reserve.

Mix together the soy sauce, lemon juice, sugar, chilli sauce and sesame oil and reserve.

Add the ginger to the wok and stir-fry for 30 seconds. Add the garlic and chilli and stir-fry for 30 seconds. Add the reserved broccoli and stir-fry for 3 minutes. Stir in the mangetout, pork and reserved noodles with the beaten eggs and water chestnuts and stir-fry for 5 minutes or until heated through. Pour over the reserved chilli sauce, toss well and turn into a warmed serving dish. Garnish and serve immediately.

Hoisin Pork

Serves 4

1.4 kg/3 lb piece lean belly
pork, boned
sea salt
2 tsp Chinese five-spice powder
2 garlic cloves, peeled and chopped
1 tsp sesame oil
4 tbsp hoisin sauce
1 tbsp clear honey
assorted salad leaves, to garnish

Preheat the oven to 200°C/400°F/Gas Mark 6, 15 minutes before cooking. Using a sharp knife, cut the pork skin in a crisscross pattern, making sure not to cut all the way through into the flesh. Rub the salt evenly over the skin and leave to stand for 30 minutes.

Meanwhile, mix together the five-spice powder, garlic, sesame oil, hoisin sauce and honey until smooth. Rub the mixture evenly over the pork skin. Place the pork on a plate and chill in the refrigerator to marinate for up to 6 hours.

Place the pork on a wire rack set inside a roasting tin and roast the pork in the preheated oven for 1–1^1/$_4$ hours, or until the pork is very crisp and the juices run clear when pierced with a skewer.

Remove the pork from the heat, leave to rest for 15 minutes, then cut into strips. Arrange on a warmed serving platter. Garnish with salad leaves and serve immediately.

Pork with Black Bean Sauce

Serves 4

700 g/1½ lb pork tenderloin
4 tbsp light soy sauce
2 tbsp groundnut oil
1 garlic clove, peeled and chopped
2.5 cm/1 inch piece fresh root ginger,
peeled and cut into matchsticks
1 large carrot, peeled and sliced
1 red pepper, deseeded and sliced
1 green pepper, deseeded
and sliced
160 g jar black bean sauce
salt
snipped fresh chives, to garnish
freshly steamed rice, to serve

Using a sharp knife, trim the pork, discarding any fat or sinew and cut into bite-sized chunks. Place in a large shallow dish and spoon over the soy sauce. Turn to coat evenly, cover with clingfilm and leave to marinate in the refrigerator for at least 30 minutes. When ready to use, lift the pork from the marinade, shaking off as much marinade as possible, and pat dry with absorbent kitchen paper. Reserve the marinade.

Heat a wok, add the groundnut oil and when hot, add the chopped garlic and ginger and stir-fry for 30 seconds. Add the carrot and the red and green peppers and stir-fry for a further 3–4 minutes or until just softened.

Add the pork to the wok and stir-fry for 5–7 minutes, or until browned all over and tender. Pour in the reserved marinade and black bean sauce. Bring to the boil, stirring constantly until well blended, then simmer for 1 minute, until heated through thoroughly. Tip into a warmed serving dish or spoon on to individual plates. Garnish with snipped chives and serve immediately with steamed rice.

Crispy Pork with Tangy Sauce

Serves 4

350 g/12 oz pork fillet
1 tbsp light soy sauce
1 tbsp dry sherry
salt and freshly ground black pepper
1 tbsp sherry vinegar
1 tbsp tomato paste
1 tbsp dark soy sauce
2 tsp light muscovado sugar
150 ml/1¼ pint chicken stock
1½ tsp clear honey
8 tsp cornflour
450 ml/¾ pint groundnut oil,
for frying
1 medium egg

To garnish:

fresh sprigs dill
orange wedges

Remove and discard any fat and sinew from the pork fillet, then cut into 2 cm/¾ inch cubes and place in a shallow dish. Blend the light soy sauce with the dry sherry and add the seasoning. Pour over the pork and stir until the pork is lightly coated. Cover and leave to marinate in the refrigerator for at least 30 minutes, stirring occasionally.

Meanwhile, blend the sherry vinegar, tomato paste, dark soy sauce, light muscovado sugar, chicken stock and honey together in a small saucepan and heat gently, stirring occasionally, until the sugar has dissolved. Then bring to the boil.

Blend 2 teaspoons of cornflour with 1 tablespoon of water and stir into the sauce. Cook, stirring, until smooth and thickened, and either keep warm or reheat when required.

Heat the oil in the wok to 190°C/375°F. Whisk together the remaining 6 teaspoons of cornflour and the egg to make a smooth batter. Drain the pork if necessary, then dip the pieces into the batter, allowing any excess to drip back into the bowl. Cook in the hot oil for 2–3 minutes, or until golden and tender. Drain on kitchen paper. Cook the pork in batches until it is all cooked, then garnish and serve immediately with the sauce.

Dim Sum Pork Parcels

Serves 40

125 g/4 oz canned water chestnuts, drained and finely chopped
125 g/4 oz raw prawns, peeled, deveined and coarsely chopped
350 g/12 oz fresh pork mince
2 tbsp smoked bacon, finely chopped
1 tbsp light soy sauce, plus extra, to serve
1 tsp dark soy sauce
1 tbsp Chinese rice wine
2 tbsp fresh root ginger, peeled and finely chopped
3 spring onions, trimmed and finely chopped
2 tsp sesame oil
1 medium egg white, lightly beaten
salt and freshly ground black pepper
2 tsp sugar
40 wonton skins, thawed if frozen
toasted sesame seeds, to garnish
soy sauce, to serve

Place the water chestnuts, prawns, pork mince and bacon in a bowl and mix together. Add the soy sauces, Chinese rice wine, ginger, chopped spring onion, sesame oil and egg white. Season to taste with salt and pepper, sprinkle in the sugar and mix the filling thoroughly.

Place a spoonful of filling in the centre of a wonton skin. Bring the sides up and press around the filling to make a basket shape. Flatten the base of the skin, so the wonton stands solid. The top should be wide open, exposing the filling.

Place the parcels on a heatproof plate, on a wire rack inside a wok or on the base of a muslin-lined bamboo steamer. Place over a wok, half-filled with boiling water, cover, then steam the parcels for about 20 minutes. Do this in two batches. Transfer to a warmed serving plate, sprinkle with toasted sesame seeds, drizzle with soy sauce and serve immediately.

Special Fried Rice

Serves 4

25 g/1 oz butter
4 medium eggs, beaten
4 tbsp vegetable oil
1 bunch spring onions, trimmed
and shredded
225 g/8 oz cooked ham, diced
125 g/4 oz large cooked prawns,
with tails left on
75 g/3 oz peas, thawed if frozen
200 g can water chestnuts, drained
and roughly chopped
450 g/1 lb cooked long-grain rice
3 tbsp dark soy sauce
1 tbsp dry sherry
2 tbsp freshly chopped coriander
salt and freshly ground black pepper

Melt the butter in a wok or large frying pan and pour in half the beaten egg. Cook for 4 minutes drawing the edges of the omelette in to allow the uncooked egg to set into a round shape. Using a fish slice, lift the omelette from the wok and roll into a sausage shape. Leave to cool completely then using a sharp knife slice the omelette into rings.

Wipe the wok with absorbent kitchen paper and return to the heat. Add the oil and when hot, add the spring onions, ham, prawns, peas and chopped water chestnuts and stir-fry for 2 minutes. Add the rice and stir-fry for a further 3 minutes.

Add the remaining beaten eggs and stir-fry for 3 minutes, or until the egg has scrambled and set. Stir in the soy sauce, sherry and chopped coriander. Season to taste with salt and pepper and heat through thoroughly. Add the omelette rings and gently stir without breaking up the egg too much. Serve immediately.

Sweet-&-Sour Spareribs

Serves 4

1.6 kg/3¹/₂ lb pork spareribs
4 tbsp clear honey
1 tbsp Worcestershire sauce
1 tsp Chinese five-spice powder
4 tbsp soy sauce
2¹/₂ tbsp dry sherry
1 tsp chilli sauce
2 garlic cloves, peeled and chopped
1¹/₂ tbsp tomato purée
1 tsp dry mustard powder (optional)
spring onion curls, to garnish

Preheat the oven to 200°C/400°F/Gas Mark 6, 15 minutes before cooking. If necessary, place the ribs on a chopping board and using a sharp knife, cut the joint in between the ribs, to form single ribs. Place the ribs in a shallow dish in a single layer.

Spoon the honey, the Worcestershire sauce, Chinese five-spice powder with the soy sauce, sherry and chilli sauce into a small saucepan and heat gently, stirring until smooth. Stir in the chopped garlic, the tomato purée and mustard powder, if using.

Pour the honey mixture over the ribs and spoon over until they are coated evenly. Cover with clingfilm and leave to marinate overnight in the refrigerator, occasionally spooning the marinade over the ribs.

When ready to cook, remove the ribs from the marinade and place in a shallow roasting tin. Spoon over a little of the marinade and reserve the remainder. Place the ribs in the preheated oven and cook for 35–40 minutes, or until cooked and the outsides are crisp. Baste occasionally with the reserved marinade during cooking. Garnish with a few spring onion curls and serve immediately, either as a starter or as a meat accompaniment.

Stir-fried Beef with Vermouth

Serves 4

350 g/12 oz beef steak, such as
rump or sirloin
2 tbsp plain flour
salt and freshly ground
black pepper
3 tbsp sunflower oil
2 shallots, peeled and
finely chopped
125 g/4 oz button mushrooms,
wiped and halved
2 tbsp freshly chopped tarragon
3 tbsp dry vermouth
150 ml/¼ pint single cream
125 g/4 oz stir-fry noodles
2 tsp sesame oil

Trim the beef and cut into thin strips. Place the flour in a bowl and add salt and pepper to taste, then stir well. Add the beef and stir until well coated, then remove from the flour and reserve.

Heat a wok, then add the oil and when hot, add the shallots and stir-fry for 2 minutes. Add the beef strips and stir-fry for 3–4 minutes before adding the mushrooms and 1 tablespoon of the chopped tarragon. Stir-fry for a further 1 minute.

Pour in the vermouth or Martini, stirring continuously, then add the cream. Cook for 2–3 minutes, or until the sauce is slightly thickened and the meat is cooked thoroughly. Adjust the seasoning and keep warm.

Meanwhile, place the noodles in a saucepan and cover with boiling water. Leave to stand for 4 minutes, then drain thoroughly and return to the wok. Add the sesame oil to the noodles and stir-fry for 1–2 minutes, or until heated through thoroughly. Pile the noodles onto serving dishes, top with the beef and serve immediately.

Beef Curry with Lemon & Arborio Rice

Serves 4

450 g/1 lb beef fillet
1 tbsp olive oil
2 tbsp green curry paste
1 green pepper, deseeded and
cut into strips
1 red pepper, deseeded and
cut into strips
1 celery stick, trimmed and sliced
juice of 1 fresh lemon
2 tsp Thai fish sauce
2 tsp demerara sugar
225 g/8 oz Arborio rice
15 g/¹/₂ oz butter
2 tbsp freshly chopped coriander
4 tbsp crème fraîche

Trim the beef fillet, discarding any fat, then cut across the grain into thin slices. Heat a wok, add the oil and when hot, add the green curry paste and cook for 30 seconds. Add the beef strips and stir-fry for 3–4 minutes.

Add the sliced peppers and the celery and continue to stir-fry for 2 minutes. Add the lemon juice, Thai fish sauce and sugar and cook for a further 3–4 minutes, or until the beef is tender and cooked to personal preference.

Meanwhile, cook the Arborio rice in a saucepan of lightly salted boiling water for 15–20 minutes, or until tender. Drain, rinse with boiling water and drain again. Return to the saucepan and add the butter. Cover and allow the butter to melt before turning it out onto a large serving dish. Sprinkle the cooked curry with the chopped coriander and serve immediately with the rice and crème fraîche.

Malaysian Beef Satay

Serves 4–6

8 wooden kebab skewers
450 g/1 lb beef steak,
such as rump or sirloin
1 tbsp vegetable oil
1 tsp fennel seeds
1 tsp fenugreek seeds
2 red chillies, deseeded
and chopped
2 garlic cloves, peeled and crushed
1 tbsp Thai red curry paste
200 ml/7 fl oz coconut milk

For the satay sauce:

1 small red chilli, deseeded and
finely chopped
1 tbsp lime juice
50 ml/2 fl oz fish sauce
2 tbsp smooth peanut butter
1 tbsp roasted peanuts,
finely chopped
2 spring onions, trimmed and
finely chopped

Soak the wooden skewers in cold water for 30 minutes. Meanwhile, trim the steak, cut into narrow strips and place in a shallow dish.

Heat the oil in a small frying pan, add the seeds and fry for 30 seconds, or until they pop. Add the chillies, crushed garlic and curry paste and continue to fry, stirring, for 2 minutes. Remove from the heat and gradually blend in the coconut milk and allow to cool. Pour over the beef, cover lightly and leave to marinate in the refrigerator for at least 30 minutes.

When ready to cook, preheat the grill to high and line the grill rack with foil. Drain the skewers and beef, reserving the remaining marinade. Thread the beef strips onto the skewers and place under the preheated grill for 8–10 minutes, or until cooked to personal preference, brushing occasionally with the remaining marinade.

Meanwhile, place all the ingredients for the sauce in a small saucepan and heat gently for 3–5 minutes, stirring occasionally until thoroughly combined and heated through.

Place the skewers on a plate, spoon over the satay sauce and garnish with lime wedges and salad, if liked.

Fried Rice with Chilli Beef

Serves 4

225 g/8 oz beef fillet
375 g/12 oz long-grain rice
4 tbsp groundnut oil
3 onions, peeled and thinly sliced
2 hot red chillies, deseeded and
finely chopped
2 tbsp light soy sauce
2 tsp tomato paste
salt and freshly ground
black pepper
2 tbsp milk
2 tbsp flour
15 g/^{1}/$_2$ oz butter
2 medium eggs

Trim the beef fillet, discarding any fat, then cut into thin strips and reserve. Cook the rice in boiling salted water for 15 minutes or according to packet instructions, then drain and reserve.

Heat a wok and add 3 tablespoons of oil. When hot, add two of the sliced onions and stir-fry for 2–3 minutes. Add the beef to the wok, together with the chopped chillies, and stir-fry for a further 3 minutes, or until tender.

Add the rice to the wok with the soy sauce and tomato paste. Stir-fry for 1–2 minutes, or until piping hot. Season to taste with salt and pepper and keep warm. Meanwhile, toss the remaining onion in the milk, then the flour in batches. In a small frying pan fry the onion in the last 1 tablespoon of oil until crisp, then reserve.

Melt the butter in a small omelette pan. Beat the eggs together with 2 teaspoons of water and pour into the pan. Cook gently, stirring frequently, until the egg has set, forming an omelette, then slide onto a clean chopping board and cut into thin strips. Add to the fried rice, sprinkle with the crispy onion and serve immediately.

Vietnamese-style Aromatic Beef

Serves 4–6

550 g/1¹/₄ lb stewing steak
2 tbsp vegetable oil
5 cardamom pods, cracked
1 cinnamon stick, bruised
3 whole star anise
2 lemon grass stalks, outer leaves
discarded and bruised
1 small green chilli, deseeded
and chopped
1–2 tbsp medium hot curry paste
2 red onions, peeled and cut
into wedges
2 garlic cloves, peeled and sliced
450 ml/³/₄ pint beef stock
150 ml/¹/₄ pint coconut milk
1 tbsp soy sauce
225 g/8 oz carrots, peeled
and sliced
175 g/6 oz sugar snap peas

Trim the meat, cut into bite-sized chunks and reserve. Heat the oil in a large heavy-based frying pan, add the cardamom pods, cinnamon stick, star anise and lemon grass and gently fry for 2 minutes. Add the chilli and continue to fry for a further 2 minutes.

Add the meat to the pan and stir-fry for 5 minutes, or until the meat is sealed.

Add the curry paste and the onions and garlic and fry for a further 5 minutes before stirring in the beef stock and coconut milk.

Bring to the boil, then reduce the heat, cover and simmer for 1¹/₂ hours, stirring occasionally. Add the soy sauce and carrots and continue to cook for a further 30 minutes. Add the sugar snap peas and cook for 10 minutes, or until the meat and vegetables are tender. Remove the cinnamon stick and whole anise and serve.

Massaman Beef Curry

Serves 4–6

450 g/1 lb beef steak, such as
sirloin or rump
3 tbsp vegetable oil
5 cm/2 inch piece fresh root ginger,
peeled and grated
3 green bird's eye chillies,
deseeded and chopped
2 red onions, peeled and chopped
3 garlic cloves, peeled and crushed
2 tbsp Massaman Thai curry paste
400 ml/14 fl oz coconut milk
150–200 ml/5–7 fl oz beef stock
350 g/12 oz new potatoes, scrubbed
and cut into small chunks
1 green pepper, deseeded and
cut into strips
50 g/2 oz roasted peanuts, chopped

Trim the beef, cut into thin strips and reserve. Heat 2 tablespoons of the oil in a heavy-based saucepan, add the ginger and chillies and fry for 3 minutes. Add the onions and garlic and continue to fry for 5 minutes, or until the onions have softened.

Remove the onions and garlic with a slotted spoon and add the beef to the pan. Cook, stirring, for 5 minutes, or until sealed.

Add the curry paste and continue to fry for 3 minutes, then return the onions and garlic to the pan and stir well.

Pour the coconut milk and stock into the pan and bring to the boil. Reduce the heat, cover and simmer for 30 minutes, stirring occasionally.

Add the potatoes to the pan, with more stock if necessary, then continue to simmer for 20–25 minutes, or until the meat and potatoes are cooked. Meanwhile, heat the remaining oil in a small saucepan, add the green pepper strips and fry for 2 minutes. Add the chopped peanuts and fry for 1 minute, stirring constantly. Sprinkle over the cooked curry and serve.

Thai Beef Curry

Serves 4–6

550 g/1¼ lb stewing beef
2 tbsp vegetable oil
1–2 bird's eye chillies, deseeded
2–3 garlic cloves,
peeled and chopped
5 cm/2 inch piece fresh root ginger,
peeled and grated
2–3 tsp Thai green curry paste,
or to taste
2 onions, peeled and chopped
2 tbsp lime juice
450 ml/¾ pint beef stock
300 ml/½ pint coconut milk
1 tsp soy sauce
1 tbsp fish sauce
1–2 tsp sugar
2 tbsp freshly chopped coriander
freshly cooked egg noodles, to serve

Trim the beef discarding any fat and gristle, cut into bite-sized chunks and reserve. Heat the oil in a heavy-based saucepan, add the chillies, garlic and ginger and fry for 2 minutes. Add the Thai green curry paste and onions and fry for 5 minutes, or until the onion has begun to soften.

Add the beef to the pan and continue to fry for a further 5 minutes, or until sealed and lightly coated in the spices.

Pour in the lime juice, stock and coconut milk, then add the soy and fish sauces. Stir and add the sugar. Bring to the boil, reduce the heat, cover and simmer, stirring occasionally, for 2 hours, or until the meat is tender. Sprinkle with chopped coriander and serve with freshly cooked noodles.

Szechuan Beef

Serves 4

450 g/1 lb beef fillet
3 tbsp hoisin sauce
2 tbsp yellow bean sauce
2 tbsp dry sherry
1 tbsp brandy
2 tbsp groundnut oil
2 red chillies, deseeded and sliced
8 bunches spring onions, trimmed and chopped
2 garlic cloves, peeled and chopped
2.5 cm/1 inch piece fresh root ginger, peeled and cut into matchsticks
1 carrot, peeled, sliced lengthways and cut into short lengths
2 green peppers, deseeded and cut into 2.5 cm/1 inch pieces
227 g can water chestnuts, drained and halved
sprigs fresh coriander, to garnish
freshly cooked noodles with freshly ground Szechuan peppercorns, to serve

Trim the beef, discarding any sinew or fat, then cut into 5 mm/¼ inch strips. Place in a large shallow dish. In a bowl, stir the hoisin sauce, yellow bean sauce, sherry and brandy together until well blended. Pour over the beef and turn until coated evenly. Cover with clingfilm and leave to marinate for at least 30 minutes.

Heat a wok or large frying pan, add the oil and when hot, add the chillies, spring onions, garlic and ginger and stir-fry for 2 minutes or until softened. Using a slotted spoon, transfer to a plate and keep warm.

Add the carrot and peppers to the wok and stir-fry for 4 minutes or until slightly softened. Transfer to a plate and keep warm.

Drain the beef, reserving the marinade, add to the wok and stir-fry for 3–5 minutes or until browned. Return the chilli mixture, the carrot and pepper mixture and the marinade to the wok, add the water chestnuts and stir-fry for 2 minutes or until heated through. Garnish with sprigs of coriander and serve immediately with the noodles.

Chicken & Lamb Satay

Serves 16

225 g/8 oz skinless, boneless chicken
225 g/8 oz lean lamb

For the marinade:

1 small onion, peeled and finely chopped
2 garlic cloves, peeled and crushed
2.5 cm/1 inch piece fresh root ginger,
peeled and grated
4 tbsp soy sauce
1 tsp ground coriander
2 tsp dark brown sugar
2 tbsp lime juice
1 tbsp vegetable oil

For the peanut sauce:

300 ml/¹/₂ pint coconut milk
4 tbsp crunchy peanut butter
1 tbsp Thai fish sauce
1 tsp lime juice
1 tbsp each chilli powder and brown sugar
salt and freshly ground black pepper

To garnish:

fresh coriander, lime wedges,

Preheat the grill just before cooking. Soak the bamboo skewers for 30 minutes before required. Cut the chicken and lamb into thin strips, about 7.5 cm/3 inches long and place in 2 shallow dishes. Blend all the marinade ingredients together, then pour half over the chicken and half over the lamb. Stir until lightly coated, then cover with clingfilm and leave to marinate in the refrigerator for at least 2 hours, turning occasionally.

Remove the chicken and lamb from the marinade and thread on to the skewers. Reserve the marinade. Cook under the preheated grill for 8–10 minutes or until cooked, turning and brushing with the marinade.

Meanwhile, make the peanut sauce. Blend the coconut milk with the peanut butter, fish sauce, lime juice, chilli powder and sugar. Pour into a saucepan and cook gently for 5 minutes, stirring occasionally, then season to taste with salt and pepper. Garnish with coriander sprigs and lime wedges and serve the satays with the prepared sauce.

Poultry

Whether it be chicken, turkey or duck, poultry is a popular base for many delicious South-East Asian dishes. Alongside classic favourites such as Pad Thai and Red Chicken Curry, this chapter is full of less familiar recipe ideas. If spicy is your style, then the Spicy Vietnamese Chicken is sure to be a hit, whilst the Lime & Sesame Turkey is a culinary experience not to be missed.

Chinese-glazed Poussin with Green & Black Rice

Serves 4

4 oven-ready poussins
salt and freshly ground black pepper
300 ml/^{1}/$_2$ pint apple juice
1 cinnamon stick
2 star anise
^{1}/$_2$ tsp Chinese five-spice powder
50 g/2 oz dark muscovado sugar
2 tbsp tomato ketchup
1 tbsp cider vinegar
grated zest of 1 orange
350 g/12 oz mixed white basmati
and wild rice
125 g/4 oz mangetout,
finely sliced lengthways
1 bunch spring onions, trimmed and
finely shredded lengthways
salt and freshly ground black pepper

Preheat the oven to 200°C/400°F/Gas Mark 6, 15 minutes before cooking. Rinse the poussins inside and out and pat dry with absorbent kitchen paper. Using tweezers, remove any feathers. Season well with salt and pepper, then reserve.

Pour the apple juice into a small saucepan and add the cinnamon stick, star anise and Chinese five-spice powder. Bring to the boil, then simmer rapidly until reduced by half. Reduce the heat, stir in the sugar, tomato ketchup, vinegar and orange zest and simmer gently until the sugar is dissolved and the glaze is syrupy. Remove from the heat and leave to cool completely. Remove the whole spices.

Place the poussins on a wire rack set over a kitchen foil-lined roasting tin. Brush generously with the apple glaze. Roast in the preheated oven for 40–45 minutes, or until the juices run clear when the thigh is pierced with a skewer, basting once or twice with the remaining glaze. Remove the poussins from the oven and leave to cool slightly.

Meanwhile, cook the rice according to the packet instructions. Bring a large saucepan of lightly salted water to the boil and add the mangetout. Blanch for 1 minute, then drain thoroughly. As soon as the rice is cooked, drain and transfer to a warmed bowl. Add the mangetout and spring onions, season to taste and stir well. Arrange on warmed dinner plates, place a poussin on top and serve immediately.

Pad Thai

Serves 4

225 g/8 oz flat rice noodles
2 tbsp vegetable oil
225 g/8 oz boneless chicken breast,
skinned and thinly sliced
4 shallots, peeled and thinly sliced
2 garlic cloves, peeled and
finely chopped
4 spring onions, trimmed and cut
into 5 cm/2 inch pieces
350 g/12 oz fresh white crab meat or
tiny prawns
75 g/3 oz fresh bean sprouts,
rinsed and drained
2 tbsp preserved or fresh
radish, chopped
2–3 tbsp roasted peanuts, chopped

For the sauce:
3 tbsp Thai fish sauce (nam pla)
2–3 tbsp rice vinegar or cider vinegar
1 tbsp each chilli bean or oyster sauce,
toasted sesame oil and brown sugar
1 red chilli, deseeded and thinly sliced

To make the sauce, whisk all the sauce ingredients in a bowl and reserve. Put the rice noodles in a large bowl and pour over enough hot water to cover. Leave to stand for about 15 minutes until softened. Drain and rinse, then drain again.

Heat the oil in a wok over a high heat until hot, but not smoking. Add the chicken strips and stir-fry constantly until they begin to colour. Using a slotted spoon, transfer to a plate. Reduce the heat to medium-high.

Add the shallots, garlic and spring onions and stir-fry for 1 minute. Stir in the rice noodles, then the reserved sauce; mix well.

Add the reserved chicken strips, with the crab meat or prawns, bean sprouts and radish and stir well. Cook for about 5 minutes, stirring frequently, until heated through. If the noodles begin to stick, add a little water.

Turn into a large shallow serving dish and sprinkle with the chopped peanuts, if desired. Serve immediately.

Spicy Vietnamese Chicken

Serves 4–6

8 small skinless, boneless chicken
breasts cut in half, about
350 g/¹/₂ oz in weight
2 lemon grass stalks, crushed and
outer leaves discarded
1 cinnamon stick, bruised
5 cm/2 inch piece fresh root ginger,
peeled and grated
2 tbsp groundnut oil
5 garlic cloves, peeled and sliced
2 red onions, peeled and
sliced into wedges
1–2 green chillies,
deseeded and chopped
freshly ground black pepper
2 tsp demerara sugar
1 tbsp light soy sauce
1 tbsp fish sauce
6 tbsp water
6 spring onions, trimmed and
diagonally sliced
100 g/4 oz roasted peanuts
freshly cooked fragrant rice, to serve

Lightly rinse the chicken portions, pat dry with absorbent kitchen paper and place in a bowl. Add the lemon grass, cinnamon stick and grated ginger, then stir well, cover and leave to chill in the refrigerator for 30 minutes.

Heat a wok or large frying pan, add the oil and, when hot, add the chicken and marinade. Cook for 5 minutes, or until browned.

Add the garlic, onions and chillies and continue to cook for a further 5 minutes.

Add the black pepper, sugar, soy sauce, fish sauce and water and cook for 10 minutes. Add the spring onions and peanuts and cook for 1 minute, then serve immediately with the cooked rice.

Baked Thai Chicken Wings

Serves 4

4 tbsp clear honey

1 tbsp chilli sauce

1 garlic clove, peeled and crushed

1 tsp freshly grated root ginger

1 lemon grass stalk, outer leaves
discarded and finely chopped

2 tbsp lime zest

3–4 tbsp freshly squeezed lime juice

1 tbsp light soy sauce

1 tsp ground cumin

1 tsp ground coriander

¼ tsp ground cinnamon

1.4 kg/3 lb chicken wings
(about 12 large wings)

6 tbsp mayonnaise

2 tbsp freshly chopped coriander

lemon or lime wedges, to garnish

Preheat the oven to 190°C/375°F/Gas Mark 5, 10 minutes before cooking. In a small saucepan, mix together the honey, chilli sauce, garlic, ginger, lemon grass, 1 tablespoon of the lime zest and 2 tablespoons of the lime juice with the soy sauce, cumin, coriander and cinnamon. Heat gently until just starting to bubble, then remove from the heat and leave to cool.

Prepare the chicken wings by folding the tips back under the thickest part of the meat to form a triangle. Arrange in a shallow ovenproof dish. Pour over the honey mixture, turning the wings to ensure that they are all well coated. Cover with clingfilm and leave to marinate in the refrigerator for 4 hours or overnight, turning once or twice.

Mix together the mayonnaise with the remaining lime zest and juice and the coriander. Leave to let the flavours develop while the wings are cooking.

Arrange the wings on a rack set over a foil-lined roasting tin. Roast at the top of the preheated oven for 50–60 minutes, or until the wings are tender and golden, basting once or twice with the remaining marinade and turning once. Remove from the oven. Garnish the wings with lemon or lime wedges and serve immediately with the mayonnaise.

Thai Stuffed Omelette

Serves 4

1 shallot, peeled and chopped
1 garlic clove, peeled and
roughly chopped
1 small red chilli, deseeded and
roughly chopped
15 g/^{1}/$_2$ oz coriander leaves
pinch sugar
2 tsp light soy sauce
2 tsp Thai fish sauce
4 tbsp vegetable or groundnut oil
175 g/6 oz skinless, boneless
chicken breast, finely sliced
^{1}/$_2$ small aubergine, diced
50 g/2 oz button or shiitake
mushrooms, wiped and sliced
^{1}/$_2$ small red pepper,
deseeded and sliced
50 g/2 oz fine green beans,
trimmed and halved
2 spring onions, trimmed and sliced
25 g/1 oz peas, thawed if frozen
6 medium eggs
salt and freshly ground black pepper
sprig fresh basil, to garnish

Place the shallot, garlic, chilli, coriander and sugar in the bowl of a spice grinder or food processor. Blend until finely chopped. Add the soy sauce, fish sauce and 1 tablespoon of the vegetable oil and blend briefly to mix into a paste. Reserve.

Heat a wok or large frying pan, add 1 tablespoon of the oil and when hot, add the chicken and aubergine and stir-fry for 3–4 minutes, or until golden. Add the mushrooms, red pepper, green beans and spring onions and stir-fry for 3–4 minutes or until tender, adding the peas for the final 1 minute. Remove from the heat and stir in the reserved coriander paste. Reserve.

Beat the eggs in a bowl and season to taste with salt and pepper. Heat the remaining oil in a large nonstick frying pan and add the eggs, tilting the pan so that the eggs cover the bottom. Stir the eggs until they are starting to set all over, then cook for 1–2 minutes, or until firm and set on the bottom but still slightly soft on top.

Spoon the chicken and vegetable mixture on to one half of the omelette and carefully flip the other half over. Cook over a low heat for 2–3 minutes, or until the omelette is set and the chicken and vegetables are heated through. Garnish with a sprig of basil and serve immediately.

Singapore Noodles

Serves 4

225 g/8 oz flat rice noodles
3 tbsp sunflower oil
2 shallots, peeled and sliced
2 garlic cloves, peeled and crushed
2 tbsp freshly grated root ginger
1 red pepper, deseeded and
finely sliced
1 hot red chilli, deseeded and
finely chopped
175 g/6 oz peeled raw prawns
125 g/4 oz boneless pork, diced
175 g/6 oz boneless chicken, diced
1 tbsp curry powder
1 tsp each crushed fennel seeds
and ground cinnamon
50 g/2 oz frozen peas, thawed
juice of 1 lemon
3 tbsp fresh coriander leaves

Put the noodles into a large bowl and pour over boiling water to cover. Leave to stand for 3 minutes, or until slightly underdone according to the packet instructions. Drain well and reserve.

Heat a wok until almost smoking. Add the oil and carefully swirl around to coat the sides of the wok. Add the shallots, garlic and ginger and cook for a few seconds. Add the pepper and chilli and stir-fry for 3–4 minutes, or until the pepper has softened.

Add the prawns, pork, chicken and curry powder to the wok. Stir-fry for a further 4–5 minutes until the meat and prawns are coloured on all sides. Then add the fennel seeds and the ground cinnamon and stir to mix.

Add the drained noodles to the wok along with the peas and cook for a further 1–2 minutes until heated through. Add the lemon juice to taste. Sprinkle with the fresh coriander leaves and serve immediately.

Thai Chicken with Chilli Peanuts

Serves 4

2 tbsp vegetable or
groundnut oil
1 garlic clove, peeled and
finely chopped
1 tsp dried chilli flakes
350 g/12 oz boneless, skinless
chicken breast, finely sliced
1 tbsp Thai fish sauce
2 tbsp peanuts, roasted and
roughly chopped
225 g/8 oz sugar snap peas
3 tbsp chicken stock
1 tbsp light soy sauce
1 tbsp dark soy sauce
large pinch sugar
freshly chopped coriander,
to garnish
boiled or steamed rice, to serve

Heat a wok or large frying pan, add the oil and when hot, carefully swirl the oil around the wok until the sides are lightly coated with the oil. Add the garlic and stir-fry for 10–20 seconds, or until starting to brown. Add the chilli flakes and stir-fry for a few seconds more.

Add the finely sliced chicken to the wok and stir-fry for 2–3 minutes, or until the chicken has turned white.

Add the following ingredients, stirring well after each addition: fish sauce, peanuts, sugar snap peas, chicken stock, light and dark soy sauces and sugar. Give a final stir.

Bring the contents of the wok to the boil, then simmer gently for 3–4 minutes, or until the chicken and vegetables are tender. Remove from the heat and tip into a warmed serving dish. Garnish with chopped coriander and serve immediately with boiled or steamed rice.

Red Chicken Curry

Serves 4

225 ml/8 fl oz coconut cream
2 tbsp vegetable oil
2 garlic clove, peeled and
finely chopped
2 tbsp Thai red curry paste
2 tbsp Thai fish sauce
2 tsp sugar
350 g/12 oz boneless, skinless
chicken breast, finely sliced
450 ml/³/₄ pint chicken stock
2 lime leaves, shredded
chopped red chilli, to garnish
freshly boiled rice or steamed Thai
fragrant rice, to serve

Pour the coconut cream into a small saucepan and heat gently. Meanwhile, heat a wok or large frying pan and add the oil. When the oil is very hot, swirl the oil around the wok until the wok is lightly coated, then add the garlic and stir-fry for about 10–20 seconds, or until the garlic begins to brown. Add the curry paste and stir-fry for a few more seconds, then pour in the warmed coconut cream.

Cook the coconut cream mixture for 5 minutes, or until the cream has curdled and thickened. Stir in the fish sauce and sugar. Add the finely sliced chicken breast and cook for 3–4 minutes, or until the chicken has turned white.

Pour the stock into the wok, bring to the boil, then simmer for 1–2 minutes, or until the chicken is cooked through. Stir in the shredded lime leaves. Turn into a warmed serving dish, garnish with chopped red chilli and serve immediately with rice.

Thai Chicken Fried Rice

Serves 4

175 g/6 oz boneless, chicken breast
2 tbsp vegetable oil
2 garlic cloves, peeled and
finely chopped
2 tsp medium curry paste
450 g/1 lb cold cooked rice
1 tbsp light soy sauce
2 tbsp Thai fish sauce
large pinch sugar
freshly ground black pepper

To garnish:

2 spring onions, trimmed and
shredded lengthways
1/2 small onion, peeled and very
finely sliced

Using a sharp knife, trim the chicken, discarding any sinew or fat and cut into small cubes. Reserve.

Heat a wok or large frying pan, add the oil and when hot, add the garlic and cook for 10–20 seconds or until just golden. Add the curry paste and stir-fry for a few seconds. Add the chicken and stir-fry for 3–4 minutes, or until tender and the chicken has turned white.

Stir the cold cooked rice into the chicken mixture, then add the soy sauce, fish sauce and sugar, stirring well after each addition. Stir-fry for 2–3 minutes, or until the chicken is cooked through and the rice is piping hot.

Check the seasoning and, if necessary, add a little extra soy sauce. Turn the rice and chicken mixture into a warmed serving dish. Season lightly with black pepper and garnish with shredded spring onion and onion slices. Serve immediately.

Stir-fried Lemon Chicken

Serves 4

350 g/12 oz boneless, skinless
chicken breast
1 large egg white
5 tsp cornflour
3 tbsp vegetable or groundnut oil
150 ml/¹/₄ pint chicken stock
2 tbsp fresh lemon juice
2 tbsp light soy sauce
1 tbsp Chinese rice wine or
dry sherry
1 tbsp sugar
2 garlic cloves, peeled and
finely chopped
¹/₄ tsp dried chilli flakes, or to taste

To garnish:

lemon rind strips
red chilli slices

Using a sharp knife, trim the chicken, discarding any fat and cut into thin strips, about 5 cm/2 inch long and 1 cm/¹/₂inch wide. Place in a shallow dish. Lightly whisk the egg white and 1 tablespoon of the cornflour together until smooth. Pour over the chicken strips and mix well until coated evenly. Leave to marinate in the refrigerator for at least 20 minutes.

When ready to cook, drain the chicken and reserve. Heat a wok or large frying pan, add the oil and when hot, add the chicken and stir-fry for 1–2 minutes, or until the chicken has turned white. Using a slotted spoon, remove from the wok and reserve.

Wipe the wok clean and return to the heat. Add the chicken stock, lemon juice, soy sauce, Chinese rice wine or sherry, sugar, garlic and chilli flakes and bring to the boil. Blend the remaining cornflour with 1 tablespoon of water and stir into the stock. Simmer for 1 minute.

Return the chicken to the wok and continue simmering for a further 2–3 minutes, or until the chicken is tender and the sauce has thickened. Garnish with the strips of lemon rind and red chilli slices. Serve immediately.

Pan-cooked Chicken with Thai Spices

Serves 4

4 kaffir lime leaves
5 cm/2 inch piece root ginger, peeled and chopped
300 ml/¹/₂ pint chicken stock, boiling
4 x 175 g/6 oz chicken breasts
2 tsp groundnut oil
5 tbsp coconut milk
1 tbsp fish sauce
2 red chillies, deseeded and finely chopped
225 g/8 oz Thai fragrant rice
1 tbsp lime juice
3 tbsp freshly chopped coriander
salt and freshly ground black pepper

To garnish:

lime wedges
freshly chopped coriander

Lightly bruise the kaffir lime leaves and put in a bowl with the chopped ginger. Pour over the chicken stock, cover and leave to infuse for 30 minutes.

Meanwhile, cut each chicken breast into two pieces. Heat the oil in a large, nonstick frying pan or flameproof casserole and brown the chicken pieces for 2–3 minutes on each side.

Strain the infused chicken stock into the pan. Half cover the pan with a lid and gently simmer for 10 minutes.

Stir in the coconut milk, fish sauce and chopped chillies. Simmer, uncovered for 5–6 minutes, or until the chicken is tender and cooked through and the sauce has reduced slightly.

Meanwhile, cook the rice in boiling salted water according to the packet instructions. Drain the rice thoroughly.

Stir the lime juice and chopped coriander into the sauce. Season to taste with salt and pepper. Serve the chicken and sauce on a bed of rice. Garnish with wedges of lime and freshly chopped coriander and serve immediately.

Chicken Chow Mein

Serves 4

225 g/8 oz egg noodles
5 tsp sesame oil
4 tsp light soy sauce
2 tbsp Chinese rice wine or
dry sherry
salt and freshly ground
black pepper
225 g/8 oz skinless chicken breast
fillets, cut into strips
3 tbsp groundnut oil
2 garlic cloves, peeled and
finely chopped
50 g/2 oz mangetout peas,
finely sliced
50 g/2 oz cooked ham, cut into
fine strips
2 tsp dark soy sauce
pinch sugar

To garnish:

shredded spring onions
toasted sesame seeds

Bring a large saucepan of water to the boil and add the noodles. Cook for 3–5 minutes, drain and plunge into cold water. Drain again, add 1 tablespoon of the sesame oil and stir lightly.

Place 2 teaspoons of light soy sauce, 1 tablespoon of Chinese rice wine or sherry, and 1 teaspoon of the sesame oil, with seasoning to taste in a bowl. Add the chicken and stir well. Cover lightly and leave to marinate in the refrigerator for about 15 minutes.

Heat the wok over a high heat, add 1 tablespoon of the groundnut oil and when very hot, add the chicken and its marinade and stir-fry for 2 minutes. Remove the chicken and juices and reserve. Wipe the wok clean with absorbent kitchen paper.

Reheat the wok and add the oil. Add the garlic and toss in the oil for 20 seconds. Add the mangetout peas and the ham and stir-fry for 1 minute. Add the noodles, remaining light soy sauce, Chinese rice wine or sherry, the dark soy sauce and sugar. Season to taste with salt and pepper and stir-fry for 2 minutes.

Add the chicken and juices to the wok and stir-fry for 4 minutes, or until the chicken is cooked. Drizzle over the remaining sesame oil. Garnish with spring onions and sesame seeds and serve.

Thai Coconut Chicken

Serves 4

1 tsp cumin seeds
1 tsp mustard seeds
1 tsp coriander seeds
1 tsp turmeric
1 bird's-eye chilli, deseeded and finely chopped
1 tbsp freshly grated root ginger
2 garlic cloves, peeled and finely chopped
125 ml/4 fl oz double cream
8 skinless chicken thighs
2 tbsp groundnut oil
1 onion, peeled and finely sliced
200 ml/7 fl oz coconut milk
salt and freshly ground black pepper
4 tbsp freshly chopped coriander
2 spring onions, shredded, to garnish
freshly cooked Thai fragrant rice, to serve

Heat the wok and add the cumin seeds, mustard seeds and coriander seeds. Dry-fry over a low to medium heat for 2 minutes, or until the fragrance becomes stronger and the seeds start to pop. Add the turmeric and leave to cool slightly. Grind the spices in a pestle and mortar or blend to a fine powder in a food processor.

Mix the chilli, ginger, garlic and the cream together in a small bowl, add the ground spices and mix. Place the chicken thighs in a shallow dish and spread the spice paste over the thighs.

Heat the wok over a high heat, add the oil and when hot, add the onion and stir-fry until golden brown. Add the chicken and spice paste. Cook for 5–6 minutes, stirring occasionally, until evenly coloured. Add the coconut milk and season to taste with salt and pepper. Simmer the chicken for 15–20 minutes, or until the thighs are cooked through, taking care not to allow the mixture to boil. Stir in the chopped coriander and serve immediately with the freshly cooked rice sprinkled with shredded spring onions.

Chinese Barbecue-style Quails with Aubergines

Serves 4

4 quails
2 tbsp salt
3 tbsp hoisin sauce
1 tbsp Chinese rice wine or dry sherry
1 tbsp light soy sauce
700 g/1½ lb aubergines, trimmed and cubed
1 tbsp oil
4 garlic cloves, peeled and finely chopped
1 tbsp freshly chopped root ginger
6 spring onions, trimmed and finely chopped
3 tbsp dark soy sauce
$1/4$ tsp dried chilli flakes
1 tbsp yellow bean sauce
1 tbsp sugar

To garnish:

sprigs of fresh coriander
sliced red chilli

Preheat the oven to 240°C/475°F/Gas Mark 9. Rub the quails inside and out with 1 tablespoon of the salt. Mix together the hoisin sauce, Chinese rice wine or sherry and light soy sauce. Rub the quails inside and out with the sauce. Transfer to a small roasting tin and roast in the preheated oven for 5 minutes. Reduce the heat to 180°C/350°F/Gas Mark 4 and continue to roast for 20 minutes. Turn the oven off and leave the quails for 5 minutes, then remove and leave to rest for 10 minutes.

Place the aubergine in a colander and sprinkle with the remaining salt. Leave to drain for 20 minutes, then rinse under cold running water and pat dry with absorbent kitchen paper.

Heat a wok or large frying pan over a moderate heat. Add the oil and when hot, add the aubergines, garlic, ginger and 4 of the spring onions and cook for 1 minute. Add the dark soy sauce, chilli flakes, yellow bean sauce, sugar and 450 ml/$3/4$ pint of water. Bring to the boil, then simmer uncovered for 10–15 minutes.

Increase the heat to high and continue to cook, stirring occasionally, until the sauce is reduced and slightly thickened. Spoon the aubergine mixture on to warmed individual plates and top with a quail. Garnish with the remaining spring onion, fresh chilli and a sprig of coriander and serve immediately.

Green Turkey Curry

Serves 4

4 baby aubergines, trimmed
and quartered
1 tsp salt
2 tbsp sunflower oil
4 shallots, peeled and halved or
quartered if large
2 garlic cloves, peeled and sliced
2 tbsp Thai green curry paste
150 ml/¼ pint chicken stock
1 tbsp Thai fish sauce
1 tbsp lemon juice
350 g/12 oz boneless, skinless
turkey breast, cubed
1 red pepper, deseeded and sliced
125 g/4 oz French beans,
trimmed and halved
25 g/1 oz creamed coconut
freshly boiled rice or steamed Thai
fragrant rice, to serve

Place the aubergines into a colander and sprinkle with
the salt. Set over a plate or in the sink to drain and leave
for 30 minutes. Rinse under cold running water and pat
dry on absorbent kitchen paper.

Heat a wok or large frying pan, add the sunflower oil
and when hot, add the shallots and garlic and stir-fry for
3 minutes, or until beginning to brown. Add the curry
paste and stir-fry for 1–2 minutes. Pour in the stock, fish
sauce and lemon juice and simmer for 10 minutes.

Add the turkey, red pepper and French beans to the wok
with the aubergines. Return to the boil, then simmer for
10–15 minutes, or until the turkey and vegetables are
tender. Add the creamed coconut and stir until melted
and the sauce has thickened. Turn into a warmed serving
dish and serve immediately with rice.

Lime Sesame Turkey

Serves 4

450 g/1 lb turkey breast, skinned
and cut into strips
2 lemon grass stalks, outer leaves
discarded and finely sliced
grated zest of 1 lime
4 garlic cloves, peeled and crushed
6 shallots, peeled and finely sliced
2 tbsp Thai fish sauce
2 tsp soft brown sugar
1 small red chilli, deseeded and
finely sliced
3 tbsp sunflower oil
1 tbsp sesame oil
225 g/8 oz stir-fry rice noodles
1 tbsp sesame seeds
shredded spring onions, to garnish
freshly stir-fried vegetables, to serve

Place the turkey strips in a shallow dish. Mix together the lemon grass stalks, lime zest, garlic, shallots, Thai fish sauce, sugar and chilli with 2 tablespoons of the sunflower oil and the sesame oil. Pour over the turkey. Cover and leave to marinate in the refrigerator for 2–3 hours, spooning the marinade over the turkey occasionally.

Soak the noodles in warm water for 5 minutes. Drain through a sieve or colander, then plunge immediately into cold water. Drain again and reserve until ready to use.

Heat the wok until very hot and add the sesame seeds. Dry-fry for 1–2 minutes, or until toasted in colour. Remove from the wok and reserve. Wipe the wok to remove any dust left from the seeds.

Heat the wok again and add the remaining sunflower oil. When hot, drain the turkey from the marinade and stir-fry for 3–4 minutes, or until golden brown and cooked through (you may need to do this in 2 batches). When all the turkey has been cooked, add the noodles to the wok and cook, stirring, for 1–2 minutes, or until heated through thoroughly. Garnish with the shredded spring onions, toasted sesame seeds and serve immediately with freshly stir-fried vegetables of your choice.

Thai Stir-fried Spicy Turkey

Serves 4

2 tbsp Thai fragrant rice
2 tbsp lemon juice
3–5 tbsp chicken stock
2 tbsp Thai fish sauce
$^{1}/_{2}$–1 tsp cayenne pepper,
or to taste
125 g/4 oz fresh turkey mince
2 shallots, peeled and chopped
$^{1}/_{2}$ lemon grass stalk, outer leaves
discarded and finely sliced
1 lime leaf, finely sliced
1 spring onion, trimmed and
finely chopped
freshly chopped coriander,
to garnish
Chinese leaves, to serve

Place the rice in a small frying pan and cook, stirring constantly, over a medium high heat for 4–5 minutes, or until the rice is browned. Transfer to a spice grinder or blender and pulse briefly until roughly ground. Reserve.

Place the lemon juice, 3 tablespoons of the stock, the fish sauce and cayenne pepper into a small saucepan and bring to the boil. Add the turkey mince and return to the boil. Continue cooking over a high heat until the turkey is sealed all over.

Add the shallots to the saucepan with the lemon grass, lime leaf, spring onion and reserved rice. Continue cooking for another 1–2 minutes, or until the turkey is cooked through, adding a little more stock, if necessary to keep the mixture moist.

Spoon a little of the mixture into each Chinese leaf and arrange on a serving dish or individual plates. Garnish with a little chopped coriander and serve immediately.

Szechuan Turkey Noodles

Serves 4

1 tbsp tomato paste

2 tsp black bean sauce

2 tsp cider vinegar

salt and freshly ground black pepper

$\frac{1}{2}$ tsp Szechuan pepper

2 tsp sugar

4 tsp sesame oil

225 g/8 oz dried egg noodles

2 tbsp groundnut oil

2 tsp freshly grated root ginger

3 garlic cloves, peeled and roughly chopped

2 shallots, peeled and finely chopped

2 courgettes, trimmed and cut into fine matchsticks

450 g/1 lb turkey breast, skinned and cut into strips

deep-fried onion rings, to garnish

Mix together the tomato paste, black bean sauce, cider vinegar, a pinch of salt and pepper, the sugar and half the sesame oil. Chill in the refrigerator for 30 minutes.

Bring a large saucepan of lightly salted water to the boil and add the noodles. Cook for 3–5 minutes, drain and plunge immediately into cold water. Toss with the remaining sesame oil and reserve.

Heat the wok until very hot, then add the oil and when hot, add the ginger, garlic and shallots. Stir-fry for 20 seconds, then add the courgettes and turkey strips. Stir-fry for 3–4 minutes, or until the turkey strips are sealed.

Add the prepared chilled black bean sauce and continue to stir-fry for another 4 minutes over a high heat. Add the drained noodles to the wok and stir until the noodles, turkey, vegetables and the sauce are well mixed together. Garnish with the deep-fried onion rings and serve immediately.

Duck in Black Bean Sauce

Serves 4

450 g/1 lb duck breast, skinned
1 tbsp light soy sauce
1 tbsp Chinese rice wine or
dry sherry
2.5 cm/1 inch piece fresh root ginger
3 garlic cloves
2 spring onions
2 tbsp Chinese preserved
black beans
1 tbsp groundnut or vegetable oil
150 ml/¼ pint chicken stock
shredded spring onions, to garnish
freshly cooked noodles, to serve

Using a sharp knife, trim the duck breasts, removing any fat. Slice thickly and place in a shallow dish. Mix together the soy sauce and Chinese rice wine or sherry and pour over the duck. Leave to marinate for 1 hour in the refrigerator, then drain and discard the marinade.

Peel the ginger and chop finely. Peel the garlic cloves and either chop finely or crush. Trim the root from the spring onions, discard the outer leaves and chop. Finely chop the black beans.

Heat a wok or large frying pan, add the oil and when very hot, add the ginger, garlic, spring onions and black beans and stir-fry for 30 seconds. Add the drained duck and stir-fry for 3–5 minutes or until the duck is browned.

Add the chicken stock to the wok, bring to the boil, then reduce the heat and simmer for 5 minutes, or until the duck is cooked and the sauce is reduced and thickened. Remove from the heat. Tip on to a bed of freshly cooked noodles, garnish with spring onion shreds and serve immediately.

Hoisin Duck Greens Stir Fry

Serves 4

350 g/12 oz duck breasts, skinned
and cut into strips
1 medium egg white, beaten
$\frac{1}{2}$ tsp salt
1 tsp sesame oil
2 tsp cornflour
2 tbsp groundnut oil
2 tbsp freshly grated root ginger
50 g/2 oz bamboo shoots
50 g/2 oz fine green beans, trimmed
50 g/2 oz pak choi, trimmed
2 tbsp hoisin sauce
1 tsp Chinese rice wine or
dry sherry
zest and juice of $\frac{1}{2}$ orange
strips of orange zest, to garnish
freshly steamed egg noodles,
to serve

Place the duck strips in a shallow dish, then add the egg white, salt, sesame oil and cornflour. Stir lightly until the duck is coated in the mixture. Cover and chill in the refrigerator for 20 minutes.

Heat the wok until very hot and add the oil. Remove the wok from the heat and add the duck, stirring continuously to prevent the duck from sticking to the wok. Add the ginger and stir-fry for 2 minutes. Add the bamboo shoots, the green beans and the pak choi, and stir-fry for 1–2 minutes until wilted.

Mix together the hoisin sauce, the Chinese rice wine or sherry and the orange zest and juice. Pour into the wok and stir to coat the duck and vegetables. Stir-fry for 1–2 minutes, or until the duck and vegetables are tender. Garnish with the strips of orange zest and serve immediately with freshly steamed egg noodles.

Crispy Aromatic Duck

Serves 4–6

2 tbsp Chinese five-spice powder
75 g/3 oz Szechuan peppercorns,
lightly crushed
25 g/1 oz whole black peppercorns,
lightly crushed
3 tbsp cumin seeds, lightly crushed
200 g/7 oz rock salt
2.7 kg/6 lb oven-ready duck
7.5 cm/3 inch piece fresh root
ginger, peeled and cut into 6 slices
6 spring onions, trimmed and
cut into 7.5 cm/3 inch lengths
cornflour for dusting
1.1 litres/2 pints groundnut oil

To serve:

warm Chinese pancakes
spring onion, cut into shreds
cucumber, cut into slices lengthways
hoisin sauce

Mix together the Chinese five-spice powder, Szechuan and black peppercorns, cumin seeds and salt. Rub the duck inside and out with the spice mixture. Wrap the duck with clingfilm and place in the refrigerator for 24 hours. Brush any loose spices from the duck. Place the ginger and spring onions into the duck cavity and put the duck on a heatproof plate.

Place a wire rack in a wok and pour in boiling water to a depth of 5 cm/2 inches. Lower the duck and plate on to the rack and cover. Steam gently for 2 hours or until the duck is cooked through, pouring off excess fat from time to time and adding more water, if necessary. Remove the duck, pour off all the liquid and discard the ginger and spring onions. Leave the duck in a cool place for 2 hours, or until it has dried and cooled.

Cut the duck into quarters and dust lightly with cornflour. Heat the oil in a wok or deep-fat fryer to 190°C/375°F, then deep-fry the duck quarters 2 at a time. Cook the breast for 8–10 minutes and the thighs and legs for 12–14 minutes, or until each piece is heated through. Drain on absorbent kitchen paper, then shred with a fork. Serve immediately with warm Chinese pancakes, spring onion shreds, cucumber slices and hoisin sauce.

Fish  Shellfish

Fish and shellfish are delicious in both curry and stir-fry dishes. Whether you prefer your fish crispy, as in Fried Fish with Thai Chilli Dipping Sauce, or delicately flaky, like the Chinese Steamed Sea Bass with Black Beans, you will find a delicious option in this chapter. If you are hoping to impress friends or family with something a little different, why not give the Scallops & Prawns Braised in Lemon Grass a try?

Thai Green Fragrant Mussels

Serves 4

2 kg/4¹/₂ lb fresh mussels
4 tbsp olive oil
2 garlic cloves, peeled and
finely sliced
3 tbsp fresh root ginger, peeled and
finely sliced
3 lemon grass stalks, outer leaves
discarded and finely sliced
1–3 red or green chillies, deseeded
and chopped
1 green pepper, deseeded
and diced
5 spring onions, trimmed and
finely sliced
3 tbsp freshly chopped coriander
1 tbsp sesame oil
juice of 3 limes
400 ml can coconut milk
warm crusty bread, to serve

Scrub the mussels under cold running water, removing any barnacles and beards. Discard any that have broken or damaged shells or are opened and do not close when tapped gently.

Heat a wok or large frying pan, add the oil and when hot, add the mussels. Shake gently and cook for 1 minute, then add the garlic, ginger, sliced lemon grass, chillies, green pepper, spring onions, 2 tablespoons of the chopped coriander and the sesame oil.

Stir-fry over a medium heat for 3–4 minutes, or until the mussels are cooked and have opened. Discard any mussels that remain unopened.

Pour the lime juice with the coconut milk into the wok and bring to the boil. Tip the mussels and the cooking liquor into warmed individual bowls. Sprinkle with the remaining chopped coriander and serve immediately with warm crusty bread.

Ginger Lobster

Serves 4

1 celery stalk, trimmed and
finely chopped
1 onion, peeled and chopped
1 small leek, trimmed and chopped
10 black peppercorns
1 x 550 g/1¹/₄ lb live lobster
25 g/1 oz butter
75 g/3 oz raw prawns, peeled and
finely chopped
6 tbsp fish stock
50 g/2 oz fresh root ginger, peeled
and cut into matchsticks
2 shallots, peeled and finely chopped
4 shiitake mushrooms, wiped and
finely chopped
1 tsp green peppercorns, drained
and crushed
2 tbsp oyster sauce
freshly ground black pepper
¹/₄ tsp cornflour
sprigs fresh coriander, to garnish
freshly cooked Thai fragrant rice and
mixed shredded leek, celery, and red
chilli, to serve

Place the celery, onion and leek in a large saucepan with the black peppercorns. Pour in 2 litres/3¹/₂ pints of hot water, bring to the boil and boil for 5 minutes, then immerse the lobster and boil for a further 8 minutes.

Remove the lobster. When cool enough to handle, sit it on its back. Using a sharp knife, halve the lobster neatly along its entire length. Remove and discard the intestinal vein from the tail, the stomach, (which lies near the head) and the inedible gills or dead man's fingers. Remove the meat from the shell and claws and cut into pieces.

Heat a wok or large frying pan, add the butter and when melted, add the raw prawns and fish stock. Stir-fry for 3 minutes or until the prawns change colour. Add the ginger, shallots, mushrooms, green peppercorns and oyster sauce. Season to taste with black pepper. Stir in the lobster. Stir-fry for 2–3 minutes.

Blend the cornflour with 1 teaspoon of water to form a thick paste, stir into the wok and cook, stirring, until the sauce thickens. Place the lobster on a warmed serving platter and tip the sauce over. Garnish and serve immediately.

Lobster Prawn Curry

Serves 4

225 g/8 oz cooked lobster meat,
shelled if necessary
225 g/8 oz raw tiger prawns,
peeled and deveined
2 tbsp groundnut oil
2 bunches spring onions,
trimmed and thickly sliced
2 garlic cloves, peeled
and chopped
2.5 cm/1 inch piece fresh root
ginger, peeled and cut
into matchsticks
2 tbsp Thai red curry paste
grated zest and juice of 1 lime
200 ml/7 fl oz coconut cream
salt and freshly ground
black pepper
3 tbsp freshly chopped coriander
freshly cooked Thai fragrant rice,
to serve

Using a sharp knife, slice the lobster meat thickly. Wash the tiger prawns and pat dry with absorbent kitchen paper. Make a small 1 cm/$\frac{1}{2}$ inch cut at the tail end of each prawn and reserve.

Heat a large wok, then add the oil and, when hot, stir-fry the lobster and tiger prawns for 4–6 minutes, or until pink. Using a slotted spoon, transfer to a plate and keep warm in a low oven.

Add the spring onions and stir-fry for 2 minutes, then stir in the garlic and ginger and stir-fry for a further 2 minutes. Add the curry paste and stir-fry for 1 minute.

Pour in the coconut cream, lime zest and juice and the seasoning. Bring to the boil and simmer for 1 minute. Return the prawns and lobster and any juices to the wok and simmer for 2 minutes. Stir in two thirds of the freshly chopped coriander to the wok mixture, then sprinkle with the remaining coriander and serve immediately.

Malaysian Fish Curry

Serves 4–6

4 firm fish fillets, such as salmon, haddock or pollack, each about 150 g/5 oz in weight
1 tbsp groundnut oil
2 garlic cloves, peeled and crushed
2.5 cm/1 inch piece fresh root ginger, peeled and grated
1 tsp turmeric
1 tsp ground coriander
2 tbsp Madras curry paste
300 ml/½ pint coconut milk
2 tbsp freshly chopped coriander
lime wedges, to garnish (optional)
stir-fried Oriental vegetables and Thai fragrant rice, to serve

Preheat the oven to 180°C/350°F/Gas Mark 4. Lightly rinse the fish fillets and pat dry with absorbent kitchen paper. Place in a lightly oiled ovenproof dish.

Heat the oil in a frying pan, add the garlic and ginger and fry for 2 minutes. Add the turmeric, ground coriander and curry paste and cook for a further 3 minutes, stirring frequently. Take off the heat and gradually stir in the coconut milk. Cool slightly then pour over the fish.

Cover with lightly buttered foil and cook in the preheated oven for 20 minutes, or until the fish is tender. Sprinkle with chopped coriander then garnish with lime wedges, if using, and serve with stir-fried vegetables and freshly cooked rice.

Fried Fish with Thai Chilli Dipping Sauce

Serves 4

1 large egg white
$^1/_2$ tsp curry powder or turmeric
3–4 tbsp cornflour
salt and freshly ground black pepper
4 plaice or sole fillets, about
225 g/8 oz each
300 ml/$^1/_2$ pint vegetable oil

For the dipping sauce:

2 red chillies, deseeded and
thinly sliced
2 shallots, peeled and
finely chopped
1 tbsp freshly squeezed lime juice
3 tbsp Thai fish sauce
1 tbsp freshly chopped coriander
or Thai basil

To serve:

freshly cooked rice
mixed salad leaves

To make the dipping sauce, combine all the ingredients in a bowl. Leave for at least 15 minutes.

Beat the egg white until frothy and whisk into a shallow dish.

Stir the curry powder or turmeric into the cornflour in a bowl and season to taste with salt and pepper. Dip each fish fillet in the beaten egg white, dust lightly on both sides with the cornflour mixture and place on a wire rack.

Heat a wok or large frying pan, add the oil and heat to 180°C/350°F. Add 1 or 2 fillets and fry for 5 minutes, or until crisp and golden, turning once during cooking.

Using a slotted spatula, carefully remove the cooked fish and place on absorbent kitchen paper to drain. Keep warm while frying the remaining fillets.

Arrange the fillets on warmed individual plates and serve immediately with the dipping sauce, rice and salad.

Fish Balls in Hot Yellow Bean Sauce

Serves 4

450 g/1 lb skinless white fish fillets, such as cod or haddock, cut into pieces

¹/₂ tsp salt

1 tbsp cornflour

2 spring onions, trimmed and chopped

1 tbsp freshly chopped coriander

1 tsp soy sauce

1 medium egg white

freshly ground black pepper

sprig tarragon, to garnish

freshly cooked rice, to serve

For the yellow bean sauce:

75 ml/3 fl oz fish or chicken stock

1–2 tsp yellow bean sauce

2 tbsp soy sauce

1–2 tbsp Chinese rice wine or dry sherry

1 tsp chilli bean sauce, or to taste

1 tsp sesame oil

1 tsp sugar (optional)

Put the fish pieces, salt, cornflour, spring onions, coriander, soy sauce and egg white into a food processor, season to taste with pepper, then blend until a smooth paste forms, scraping down the sides of the bowl occasionally.

With dampened hands, shape the mixture into 2.5 cm/1 inch balls. Transfer to a baking tray and chill in the refrigerator for at least 30 minutes.

Bring a large saucepan of water to simmering point. Working in 2 or 3 batches, drop in the fish balls and poach gently for 3–4 minutes or until they float to the top. Transfer to absorbent kitchen paper to drain.

Put all the sauce ingredients in a wok or large frying pan and bring to the boil. Add the fish balls to the sauce and stir-fry gently for 2–3 minutes until piping hot. Transfer to a warmed serving dish, garnish with the sprig of tarragon and serve immediately with freshly cooked rice.

Steamed Whole Trout with Ginger & Spring Onion

Serves 4

2 x 450–700 g/1–1½ lb whole trout, gutted with heads removed
coarse sea salt
2 tbsp groundnut oil
½ tbsp soy sauce
1 tbsp sesame oil
2 garlic cloves, peeled and thinly sliced
2.5 cm/1 inch piece fresh root ginger, peeled and thinly slivered
2 spring onions, trimmed and thinly sliced diagonally

To garnish:

chive leaves
lemon slices

To serve:

freshly cooked rice
Oriental salad, to serve

Wipe the fish inside and out with absorbent kitchen paper then rub with salt inside and out and leave for about 20 minutes. Pat dry with absorbent kitchen paper.

Set a steamer rack or inverted ramekin in a large wok and pour in enough water to come about 5 cm/2 inches up the side of the wok. Bring to the boil.

Brush a heatproof dinner plate with a little of the groundnut oil and place the fish on the plate with the tails pointing in opposite directions. Place the plate on the rack, cover tightly and simmer over a medium heat for 10–12 minutes, or until tender and the flesh is opaque near the bone.

Carefully transfer the plate to a heatproof surface. Sprinkle with the soy sauce and keep warm.

Pour the water out of the wok and return to the heat. Add the remaining groundnut and sesame oils and when hot, add the garlic, ginger and spring onion and stir-fry for 2 minutes, or until golden. Pour over the fish, garnish with chive leaves and lemon slices and serve immediately with rice and an Oriental salad.

Chinese Steamed Sea Bass
with Black Beans

Serves 4

1.1 kg/2½ lb sea bass, cleaned
with head and tail left on
1–2 tbsp rice wine or
dry sherry
1½ tbsp groundnut oil
2–3 tbsp fermented black beans,
rinsed and drained
1 garlic clove, peeled and
finely chopped
1 cm/½ inch piece fresh root ginger,
peeled and finely chopped
4 spring onions, trimmed and thinly
sliced diagonally
2–3 tbsp soy sauce
125 ml/4 fl oz fish or chicken stock
1–2 tbsp sweet Chinese chilli sauce,
or to taste
2 tsp sesame oil
sprigs fresh coriander, to garnish

Using a sharp knife, cut 3–4 deep diagonal slashes along both sides of the fish. Sprinkle the Chinese rice wine or sherry inside and over the fish and gently rub into the skin on both sides.

Lightly brush a heatproof plate large enough to fit into a large wok or frying pan with a little of the groundnut oil. Place the fish on the plate, curving the fish along the inside edge of the dish, then leave for 20 minutes.

Place a wire rack or inverted ramekin in the wok and pour in enough water to come about 2.5 cm/1 inch up the side. Bring to the boil over a high heat.

Carefully place the plate with the fish on the rack or ramekin, cover and steam for 12–15 minutes, or until the fish is tender and the flesh is opaque when pierced with a knife near the bone.

Remove the plate with the fish from the wok and keep warm. Remove the rack or ramekin from the wok and pour off the water. Return the wok to the heat, add the remaining groundnut oil and swirl to coat the bottom and side. Add the black beans, garlic and ginger and stir-fry for 1 minute.

Add the spring onions, soy sauce, fish or chicken stock and boil for 1 minute. Stir in the chilli sauce and sesame oil, then pour the sauce over the cooked fish. Garnish with coriander sprigs and serve immediately.

Fragrant Thai Swordfish with Peppers

Serves 4–6

For the marinade:

1 tbsp each of soy sauce, Chinese rice wine, sesame oil and cornflour

550 g/1¼ lb swordfish, cut into 5 cm/2 inch strips
2 tbsp vegetable oil
2 lemon grass stalks, peeled, bruised and cut into 2.5 cm/1 inch pieces
2.5 cm/1 inch piece fresh root ginger, peeled and thinly sliced
4–5 shallots, peeled and thinly sliced
2–3 garlic cloves, peeled and sliced
1 small red pepper, deseeded and thinly sliced
1 small yellow pepper, deseeded and thinly sliced
2 tbsp soy sauce
2 tbsp Chinese rice wine or dry sherry
1–2 tsp sugar
1 tsp sesame oil
1 tbsp Thai or Italian basil, shredded
salt and freshly ground black pepper
1 tbsp toasted sesame seeds

Blend all the marinade ingredients together in a shallow, nonmetallic baking dish. Add the swordfish and spoon the marinade over the fish. Cover and leave to marinate in the refrigerator for at least 30 minutes.

Using a slotted spatula or spoon, remove the swordfish from the marinade and drain briefly on absorbent kitchen paper. Heat a wok or large frying pan, add the oil and when hot, add the swordfish and stir-fry for 2 minutes, or until it begins to brown. Remove the swordfish and drain on absorbent kitchen paper.

Add the lemon grass, ginger, shallots and garlic to the wok and stir-fry for 30 seconds. Add the peppers, soy sauce, Chinese rice wine or sherry and sugar and stir-fry for 3–4 minutes.

Return the swordfish to the wok and stir-fry gently for 1–2 minutes, or until heated through and coated with the sauce. If necessary, moisten the sauce with a little of the marinade or some water. Stir in the sesame oil and the basil and season to taste with salt and pepper. Tip into a warmed serving bowl, sprinkle with sesame seeds and serve immediately.

Chinese Five-Spice Marinated Salmon

Serves 4

For the marinade:

3 tbsp soy sauce
3 tbsp Chinese rice wine or
dry sherry
2 tsp sesame oil
1 tbsp soft brown sugar
1 tbsp lime or lemon juice
1 tsp Chinese five-spice powder
2–3 dashes hot pepper sauce

700 g/1¹/₂ lb skinless salmon fillet,
cut into 2.5 cm/1 inch strips
2 medium egg whites
1 tbsp cornflour
vegetable oil for frying
4 spring onions, cut diagonally into
5 cm/2 inch pieces
125 ml/4 fl oz fish stock
lime or lemon wedges, to garnish

Combine the marinade ingredients in a shallow nonmetallic baking dish until well blended. Add the salmon strips and stir gently to coat. Leave to marinate in the refrigerator for 20–30 minutes.

Using a slotted spoon or fish slice, remove the salmon pieces, drain on absorbent kitchen paper and pat dry. Reserve the marinade.

Beat the egg whites with the cornflour to make a batter. Add the salmon strips and stir into the batter until coated completely.

Pour enough oil into a large wok to come 5 cm/2 inches up the side and place over a high heat. Working in two or three batches, add the salmon strips and cook for 1–2 minutes or until golden. Remove from the wok with a slotted spoon and drain on absorbent kitchen paper. Reserve.

Discard the hot oil and wipe the wok clean. Add the marinade, spring onions and stock to the wok. Bring to the boil and simmer for 1 minute. Add the salmon strips and stir-fry gently until coated in the sauce. Spoon into a warmed shallow serving dish, garnish with the lime or lemon wedges and serve immediately.

Seafood in Green Curry Sauce

Serves 4

175 g/6 oz cod or haddock
fillet, skinned
175 g/6 oz salmon fillet, skinned
225 g/8 oz monkfish fillet, skinned
1 tbsp vegetable oil
1 small onion, peeled and chopped
small piece fresh root ginger,
peeled and grated
2 lemon grass stalks, crushed and
outer leaves discarded
3 kaffir lime leaves
1 Thai red chilli, deseeded
and chopped
1 tbsp Thai green curry paste,
or to taste
1 tbsp light soy sauce
300 ml/¹/₂ pint coconut milk
120 ml/4 fl oz water
2 tbsp lime juice
2 tbsp freshly chopped coriander
freshly cooked Thai fragrant rice,
to serve

Remove any pin bones if necessary from the fish and cut into small chunks; reserve.

Heat the oil in a wok or large saucepan, add the onion and fry for 2 minutes, stirring frequently. Add the ginger, lemon grass, lime leaves and chopped chilli and continue to stir-fry for 3 minutes.

Add the green curry paste and soy sauce, stir well then add the coconut milk and water. Bring to the boil, then reduce the heat and simmer for 5 minutes.

Add the fish and continue to simmer for 12–15 minutes, or until the fish is cooked. Add the lime juice, stir in the chopped coriander and serve with the freshly cooked Thai fragrant rice.

Coconut Seafood

Serves 4

2 tbsp groundnut oil
450 g/1 lb raw king prawns, peeled
2 bunches spring onions, trimmed
and thickly sliced
1 garlic clove, peeled and chopped
2.5 cm/1 inch piece fresh root
ginger, peeled and cut
into matchsticks
125 g/4 oz fresh shiitake
mushrooms, rinsed and halved
150 ml/¼ pint dry white wine
200 ml/7 fl oz carton coconut cream
4 tbsp freshly chopped coriander
salt and freshly ground
black pepper
freshly cooked Thai fragrant rice

Heat a large wok, add the oil and heat until it is almost smoking, swirling the oil around the wok to coat the sides. Add the prawns and stir-fry over a high heat for 4-5 minutes, or until browned on all sides. Using a slotted spoon, transfer the prawns to a plate and keep warm in a low oven.

Add the spring onions, garlic and ginger to the wok and stir-fry for 1 minute. Add the mushrooms and stir-fry for a further 3 minutes. Using a slotted spoon, transfer the mushroom mixture to a plate and keep warm in a low oven.

Add the wine and coconut cream to the wok, bring to the boil and boil rapidly for 4 minutes, until reduced slightly.

Return the mushroom mixture and prawns to the wok, bring back to the boil, then simmer for 1 minute, stirring occasionally, until piping hot. Stir in the freshly chopped coriander and season to taste with salt and pepper. Serve immediately with the freshly cooked Thai fragrant rice.

Thai Curried Seafood

Serves 6–8

2 tbsp vegetable oil
450 g/1 lb scallops, halved if large
1 onion, peeled and finely chopped
4 garlic cloves, peeled and chopped
5 cm/2 inch piece fresh root ginger,
peeled and finely chopped
1–2 red chillies, deseeded and
thinly sliced
1–2 tbsp curry paste (strength to taste)
1 tsp each ground coriander and cumin
1 lemon grass stalk, bruised
225 g can chopped tomatoes
125 ml/4 fl oz chicken stock or water
450 ml/³/₄ pint coconut milk
12 live mussels, scrubbed and
beards removed
450 g/1 lb cooked peeled prawns
225 g/8 oz frozen or canned
crab meat, drained
2 tbsp freshly chopped coriander
freshly shredded coconut,
to garnish (optional)
freshly cooked rice or noodles, to serve

Heat a wok or large frying pan, add 1 tablespoon of the oil and when hot, add the scallops, with coral attached if preferred, and stir-fry for 2 minutes or until opaque and firm. Transfer to a plate with any juices.

Heat the remaining oil. Add the onion, garlic, ginger and chillies and stir-fry for 1 minute or until they begin to soften.

Add the curry paste, coriander, cumin and lemon grass and stir-fry for 2 minutes. Add the tomatoes and stock, bring to the boil then simmer for 5 minutes or until reduced, stirring constantly. Stir in the coconut milk and simmer for 2 minutes.

Stir in the mussels, cover and simmer for 2 minutes or until they begin to open. Stir in the prawns, crab meat and reserved scallops with any juices and cook for 2 minutes or until heated through. Discard the lemon grass and any unopened mussels. Stir in the chopped coriander. Tip into a large warmed serving dish and garnish with the coconut, if using. Serve immediately with freshly cooked rice or noodles.

Singapore-style Curry

Serves 4–6

175 g/6 oz basmati rice
450 g/1 lb large prawns, peeled
2 tbsp vegetable oil
5 cm/2 inch piece fresh root ginger,
peeled and grated
1–3 red chillies, deseeded and sliced
4 shallots, peeled and cut into
thin wedges
1 red pepper, deseeded and cut
into small chunks
1 large courgette, trimmed and cut
into chunks
2–4 tbsp sweet chilli sauce
225 g/8 oz ripe tomatoes,
peeled and chopped
2 tbsp freshly chopped coriander

Cook the rice in a saucepan of boiling water for 12–15 minutes, or until tender. Drain and keep warm. Clean the prawns, removing the thin black thread if necessary, and reserve. Heat the oil in a large pan or wok, add the ginger and chillies and fry for 1 minute.

Add the shallots and red pepper and stir-fry for 3 minutes. Add the courgette, sweet chilli sauce to taste and chopped tomatoes and simmer for 2 minutes.

Add the prawns and continue to simmer for 5 minutes, or until the prawns have turned pink.

Place a portion of cooked rice in the base of four to six deep serving bowls and spoon over some of the prawn mixture and liquor. Sprinkle each with chopped coriander and serve.

Szechuan Chilli Prawns

Serves 4

450 g/1 lb raw tiger prawns
2 tbsp groundnut oil
1 onion, peeled and sliced
1 red pepper, deseeded and cut
into strips
1 small red chilli, deseeded and
thinly sliced
2 garlic cloves, peeled and
finely chopped
2–3 spring onions, trimmed and
diagonally sliced
freshly cooked rice or noodles,
to serve
sprigs fresh coriander or chilli flowers,
to garnish

For the chilli sauce:
1 tbsp cornflour
4 tbsp cold fish stock or water
2 tbsp soy sauce
2 tbsp sweet or hot chilli sauce,
or to taste
2 tsp soft light brown sugar

Peel the prawns, leaving the tails attached if you like. Using a sharp knife, remove the black vein along the back of the prawns. Rinse and pat dry with absorbent kitchen paper.

Heat a wok or large frying pan, add the oil and when hot, add the onion, pepper and chilli and stir-fry for 4–5 minutes, or until the vegetables are tender but retain a bite. Stir in the garlic and cook for 30 seconds. Using a slotted spoon, transfer to a plate and reserve.

Add the prawns to the wok and stir-fry for 1–2 minutes, or until they turn pink and opaque.

Blend all the chilli sauce ingredients together in a bowl or jug, then stir into the prawns. Add the reserved vegetables and bring to the boil, stirring constantly. Cook for 1–2 minutes, or until the sauce is thickened and the prawns and vegetables are well coated.

Stir in the spring onions, tip on to a warmed platter and garnish with chilli flowers or coriander sprigs. Serve immediately with freshly cooked rice or noodles.

Crispy Prawn Stir-fry

Serves 4

3 tbsp soy sauce
1 tsp cornflour
pinch sugar
6 tbsp groundnut oil
450 g/1 lb raw shelled tiger prawns,
halved lengthways
125 g/4 oz carrots, peeled and cut
into matchsticks
2.5 cm/1 inch piece fresh root ginger,
peeled and cut into matchsticks
125 g/4 oz mangetout peas,
trimmed and shredded
125 g/4 oz asparagus spears, cut
into short lengths
125 g/4 oz beansprouts
1/4 head Chinese leaves, shredded
2 tsp sesame oil

Mix together the soy sauce, cornflour and sugar in a small bowl and reserve.

Heat a large wok, then add 3 tablespoons of the oil and heat until almost smoking. Add the prawns and stir-fry for 4 minutes, or until pink all over. Using a slotted spoon, transfer the prawns to a plate and keep warm in a low oven.

Add the remaining oil to the wok and when just smoking, add the carrots and ginger and stir-fry for 1 minute, or until slightly softened, then add the mangetout peas and stir-fry for a further 1 minute. Add the asparagus and stir-fry for 4 minutes, or until softened.

Add the beansprouts and Chinese leaves and stir-fry for 2 minutes, or until the leaves are slightly wilted. Pour in the soy sauce mixture and return the prawns to the wok. Stir-fry over a medium heat until piping hot, then add the sesame oil, give a final stir and serve immediately.

Thai Marinated Prawns

Serves 4

For the marinade:

2 lemon grass stalks, outer leaves
discarded and bruised
2 garlic cloves, peeled and
finely chopped
2 shallots, peeled and
finely chopped
1 red chilli, deseeded and chopped
grated zest and juice of 1 small lime
400 ml/14 fl oz coconut milk

700 g/1 1/2 lb large raw prawns,
peeled with tails left on
2 large eggs
salt
50 g/2 oz cornflour
vegetable oil for deep-frying
lime wedges, to garnish

Mix all the marinade ingredients together in a bowl, pressing on the solid ingredients to release their flavours. Season to taste with salt and reserve.

Using a sharp knife, remove the black vein along the back of the prawns and pat dry with absorbent kitchen paper. Add the prawns to the marinade and stir gently until coated evenly. Leave in the marinade for at least 1 hour, stirring occasionally.

Beat the eggs in a deep bowl with a little salt. Place the cornflour in a shallow bowl. Using a slotted spoon or spatula, transfer the prawns from the marinade to the cornflour. Stir gently until the prawns are coated on all sides and shake off any excess.

Holding each prawn by its tail, dip it into the beaten egg, then into the cornflour again, shaking off any excess.

Pour enough oil into a large wok to come 5 cm/2 inches up the sides and place over a high heat. Working in batches of five or six, deep-fry the prawns for 2 minutes, or until pink and crisp, turning once. Using a slotted spoon, remove and drain on absorbent kitchen paper. Keep warm. Arrange on a warmed serving plate and garnish with lime wedges. Serve immediately.

Red Prawn Curry with Jasmine-scented rice

Serves 4

1/2 tbsp coriander seeds
1 tsp each cumin seeds and black
peppercorns
1/2 tsp salt
1–2 dried red chillies
2 shallots, peeled and chopped
3–4 garlic cloves
2.5 cm/1 inch piece fresh galangal or
root ginger, peeled and chopped
1 kaffir lime leaf or 1 tsp kaffir lime zest
1/2 tsp red chilli powder
1/2 tbsp shrimp paste
1–1 1/2 lemon grass stalks, outer leaves
removed and thinly sliced
750 ml/1 1/4 pints coconut milk
1 red chilli deseeded and thinly sliced
2 tbsp Thai fish sauce
2 tsp soft brown sugar
1 red pepper, deseeded and sliced
550 g/1 1/4 lb peeled tiger prawns
2 fresh lime leaves, shredded
2 tbsp each fresh mint leaves and Thai
or Italian basil leaves, shredded
Thai fragrant rice, to serve

Using a pestle and mortar or a spice grinder, grind the coriander and cumin seeds, peppercorns and salt to a fine powder. Add the dried chillies one at a time and grind to a fine powder.

Place the shallots, garlic, galangal or ginger, kaffir lime leaf or zest, chilli powder and shrimp paste in a food processor. Add the ground spices and process until a thick paste forms. Scrape down the bowl once or twice, adding a few drops of water if the mixture is too thick and not forming a paste. Stir in the lemon grass.

Transfer the paste to a large wok and cook over a medium heat for 2–3 minutes or until fragrant.

Stir in the coconut milk, bring to the boil, then lower the heat and simmer for about 10 minutes. Add the chilli, fish sauce, sugar and red pepper and simmer for 15 minutes.

Stir in the prawns and cook for 5 minutes, or until the prawns are pink and tender. Stir in the shredded herbs, heat for a further minute and serve immediately with the freshly cooked rice.

Stir-fried Tiger Prawns

Serves 4

75 g/3 oz fine egg thread noodles
125 g/4 oz broccoli florets
125 g/4 oz baby sweetcorn, halved
3 tbsp soy sauce
1 tbsp lemon juice
pinch sugar
1 tsp chilli sauce
1 tsp sesame oil
2 tbsp sunflower oil
450 g/1 lb raw tiger prawns,
peeled, heads and tails
removed, and deveined
2.5 cm/1 inch piece fresh root
ginger, peeled and cut into sticks
1 garlic clove, peeled and chopped
1 red chilli, deseeded and sliced
2 medium eggs, lightly beaten
227 g can water chestnuts,
drained and sliced

Place the noodles in a large bowl, cover with plenty of boiling water and leave to stand for 5 minutes, or according to packet directions; stir occasionally. Drain and reserve. Blanch the broccoli and sweetcorn in a saucepan of boiling salted water for 2 minutes, then drain and reserve.

Meanwhile, mix together the soy sauce, lemon juice, sugar, chilli sauce and sesame oil in a bowl and reserve.

Heat a large wok, then add the sunflower oil and heat until just smoking. Add the prawns and stir-fry for 2–3 minutes, or until pink on all sides. Using a slotted spoon, transfer the prawns to a plate and reserve. Add the ginger and stir-fry for 30 seconds. Add the garlic and chilli to the wok and cook for a further 30 seconds.

Add the noodles and stir-fry for 3 minutes, until the noodles are crisp. Stir in the prawns, vegetables, eggs and water chestnuts and stir-fry for a further 3 minutes, until the eggs are lightly cooked. Pour over the chilli sauce, stir lightly and serve immediately.

Thai Coconut Crab Curry

Serves 4–6

1 onion
4 garlic cloves
5 cm/2 inch piece fresh root ginger
2 tbsp vegetable oil
2–3 tsp hot curry paste
400 g/14 oz coconut milk
2 large dressed crabs, white and
dark meat separated
2 lemon grass stalks,
peeled and bruised
6 spring onions,
trimmed and chopped
2 tbsp freshly shredded Thai basil
or mint, plus extra, to garnish
freshly boiled rice, to serve

Peel the onion and chop finely. Peel the garlic cloves, then either crush or finely chop. Peel the ginger and either grate coarsely or cut into very thin shreds. Reserve.

Heat a wok or large frying pan, add the oil and when hot, add the onion, garlic and ginger and stir-fry for 2 minutes, or until the onion is beginning to soften. Stir in the curry paste and stir-fry for 1 minute.

Stir the coconut milk into the vegetable mixture with the dark crab meat. Add the lemon grass, then bring the mixture slowly to the boil, stirring frequently.

Add the spring onions and simmer gently for 15 minutes or until the sauce has thickened. Remove and discard the lemon grass stalks.

Add the white crab meat and the shredded basil or mint and stir very gently for 1–2 minutes or until heated through and piping hot. Try to prevent the crab meat from breaking up.

Spoon the curry over boiled rice on warmed individual plates, sprinkle with basil or mint leaves and serve immediately.

Deep-fried Crab Wontons

Makes 24–30

2 tbsp sesame oil
6–8 water chestnuts, rinsed, drained and chopped
2 spring onions, peeled and finely chopped
1 cm/^{1}/$_2$ inch piece fresh root ginger, peeled and grated
185 g can white crab meat, drained
50 ml/2 fl oz soy sauce
2 tbsp rice wine vinegar
^{1}/$_2$ tsp dried crushed chillies
2 tsp sugar
^{1}/$_2$ tsp hot pepper sauce, or to taste
1 tbsp freshly chopped coriander or dill
1 large egg yolk
1 packet wonton skins
vegetable oil for deep-frying
lime wedges, to garnish
dipping sauce, to serve
(*see* page 52)

Heat a wok or large frying pan, add 1 tablespoon of the sesame oil and when hot, add the water chestnuts, spring onions and ginger and stir-fry for 1 minute. Remove from the heat and leave to cool slightly.

In a bowl, mix the crab meat with the soy sauce, rice wine vinegar, crushed chillies, sugar, hot pepper sauce, chopped coriander or dill and the egg yolk. Stir in the cooled stir-fried mixture until well blended.

Lay the wonton skins on a work surface and place 1 teaspoonful of the crab mixture on the centre of each. Brush the edges of each wonton skin with a little water and fold up one corner to the opposite corner to form a triangle. Press to seal. Bring the two corners of the triangle together to meet in the centre, brush one with a little water and overlap them, pressing to seal and form a 'tortellini' shape. Place on a baking sheet and continue with the remaining triangles.

Pour enough oil into a large wok to come 5 cm/2 inches up the sides and place over a high heat. Working in batches of five or six, fry the wontons for 3 minutes, or until crisp and golden, turning once or twice.

Carefully remove the wontons with a slotted spoon, drain on absorbent kitchen paper and keep warm. Place on individual warmed serving plates, garnish with a lime wedge and serve immediately with the dipping sauce.

Scallops with Black Bean Sauce

Serves 4

700 g/1¹/₂ lb scallops, with their coral
2 tbsp vegetable oil
2–3 tbsp Chinese fermented black
beans, rinsed, drained and
coarsely chopped
2 garlic cloves, peeled and
finely chopped
4 cm/1¹/₂ inch piece fresh
root ginger, peeled and
finely chopped
4–5 spring onions, thinly
sliced diagonally
2–3 tbsp soy sauce
1¹/₂ tbsp Chinese rice wine or
dry sherry
1–2 tsp sugar
1 tbsp fish stock or water
2–3 dashes hot pepper sauce
1 tbsp sesame oil
freshly cooked noodles, to serve

Pat the scallops dry with absorbent kitchen paper. Carefully separate the orange coral from the scallop. Peel off and discard the membrane and thickish opaque muscle that attaches the coral to the scallop. Cut any large scallops crossways in half, leave the corals whole.

Heat a wok or large frying pan, add the oil and when hot, add the white scallop meat and stir-fry for 2 minutes, or until just beginning to colour on the edges. Using a slotted spoon or spatula, transfer to a plate. Reserve.

Add the black beans, garlic and ginger and stir-fry for 1 minute. Add the spring onions, soy sauce, Chinese rice wine or sherry, sugar, fish stock or water, hot pepper sauce and the corals and stir until mixed.

Return the scallops and juices to the wok and stir-fry gently for 3 minutes, or until the scallops and corals are cooked through. Add a little more stock or water if necessary. Stir in the sesame oil and turn into a heated serving dish. Serve immediately with noodles.

Scallops Prawns Braised in Lemon Grass

Serves 4–6

450 g/1 lb large raw prawns,
peeled with tails left on
350 g/12 oz scallops, with
coral attached
2 red chillies, deseeded and
coarsely chopped
2 garlic cloves, peeled and
coarsely chopped
4 shallots, peeled
1 tbsp shrimp paste
2 tbsp freshly chopped coriander
400 ml/14 fl oz coconut milk
2–3 lemon grass stalks, outer
leaves discarded and bruised
2 tbsp Thai fish sauce
1 tbsp sugar
freshly steamed basmati rice,
to serve

Rinse the prawns and scallops and pat dry with absorbent kitchen paper. Using a sharp knife, remove the black vein along the back of the prawns. Reserve.

Place the chillies, garlic, shallots, shrimp paste and 1 tablespoon of the chopped coriander in a food processor. Add 1 tablespoon of the coconut milk and 2 tablespoons of water and blend to form a thick paste. Reserve the chilli paste.

Pour the remaining coconut milk with 3 tablespoons of water into a large wok or frying pan, add the lemon grass and bring to the boil. Simmer over a medium heat for 10 minutes or until reduced slightly.

Stir the chilli paste, fish sauce and sugar into the coconut milk and continue to simmer for 2 minutes, stirring occasionally.

Add the prepared prawns and scallops and simmer gently, for 3 minutes, stirring occasionally, or until cooked and the prawns are pink and the scallops are opaque.

Remove the lemon grass and stir in the remaining chopped coriander. Serve immediately spooned over freshly steamed basmati rice.

Oriental Spicy Scallops

Serves 6

12 fresh scallops, trimmed
12 rashers smoked streaky
bacon, derinded
2 tbsp groundnut oil
1 red onion, peeled and cut
into wedges
1 red pepper, deseeded and sliced
1 yellow pepper, deseeded
and sliced
2 garlic cloves, peeled and chopped
$\frac{1}{2}$ tsp garam masala
1 tbsp tomato paste
1 tbsp paprika
4 tbsp freshly chopped coriander

To serve:

freshly cooked noodles
Oriental-style salad

Remove the thin black thread from the scallops, rinse lightly and pat dry on absorbent kitchen paper. Wrap each scallop in a bacon rasher. Place on a baking sheet, cover and chill in the refrigerator for 30 minutes.

Meanwhile heat the wok, then add 1 tablespoon of the oil and stir-fry the onion for 3 minutes, or until almost softened. Add the peppers and stir-fry for 5 minutes, stirring occasionally, until browned. Using a slotted spoon, transfer the vegetables to a plate and reserve.

Add the remaining oil to the wok, heat until almost smoking and then add the scallops, seam-side down, and stir-fry for 2–3 minutes. Turn the scallops over and stir-fry for a further 2–3 minutes, until the bacon is crisp and the scallops are almost tender. Add the garlic, garam masala, tomato paste and paprika and stir until the scallops are lightly coated.

Stir in the remaining ingredients with the reserved vegetables. Stir-fry for a further 1–2 minutes or until the vegetables are piping hot. Serve immediately with noodles and an Oriental salad.

Vegetables

❧ Salads

There are a multitude of tasty vegetable and salad dishes that showcase the fresh flavours of South-East Asia. From cold salads to hot noodles, vegetable lovers will find it hard to choose between the recipes in this chapter! For a quick lunch rustle up the Oriental Noodle & Peanut Salad with Coriander, or for a healthy and filling main, Thai Noodles & Vegetables with Tofu is bound to go down a treat.

Prawn Salad with Toasted Rice

Serves 4

For the dressing:
50 ml/2 fl oz rice vinegar
1 red chilli, deseeded and
thinly sliced
7.5 cm/3 inch piece lemon
grass stalk, bruised
juice of 1 lime
2 tbsp Thai fish sauce
1 tsp sugar, or to taste

For the salad:
350 g/12 oz large raw prawns, peeled,
with tails attached, heads removed
cayenne pepper
1 tbsp long-grain white rice
salt and freshly ground black pepper
2 tbsp sunflower oil
1 large head Chinese leaves or
cos lettuce, shredded
1/2 small cucumber,
peeled, deseeded and thinly sliced
1 small bunch chives, cut into
2.5 cm/1 inch pieces
small bunch mint leaves

Place all the ingredients for the dressing in a small bowl and leave to stand to let the flavours blend together.

Using a sharp knife, split each prawn lengthways in half, leaving the tail attached to one half. Remove any black vein and pat the prawns dry with absorbent kitchen paper. Sprinkle the prawns with a little salt and cayenne pepper and then reserve.

Heat a wok over a high heat. Add the rice and stir-fry until browned and fragrant. Turn into a mortar and cool. Crush gently with a pestle until coarse crumbs form. Wipe the wok clean.

Reheat the wok, add the oil and when hot, add the prawns and stir-fry for 2 minutes, or until pink. Transfer to a plate and season to taste with salt and pepper.

Place the Chinese leaves or lettuce into a salad bowl with the cucumber, chives and mint leaves and toss lightly together.

Remove the lemon grass stalk and some of the chilli from the dressing and pour all but 2 tablespoons over the salad and toss until lightly coated. Add the prawns and drizzle with the remaining dressing, then sprinkle with the toasted rice and serve.

Thai Curry with Tofu

Serves 4

750 ml/1¼ pints coconut milk
700 g/1½ lb tofu, drained and cut
into small cubes
salt and freshly ground black pepper
4 garlic cloves, peeled and chopped
1 large onion, peeled and cut
into wedges
1 tsp crushed dried chillies
grated zest of 1 lemon
2.5 cm/1 inch piece fresh root
ginger, peeled and grated
1 tbsp ground coriander
1 tsp ground cumin
1 tsp turmeric
2 tbsp light soy sauce
1 tsp cornflour
Thai fragrant rice, to serve

To garnish:

2 red chillies, deseeded and cut
into rings
1 tbsp freshly chopped coriander
lemon wedges

Pour 600 ml/1 pint of the coconut milk into a saucepan and bring to the boil. Add the tofu, season to taste with salt and pepper and simmer gently for 10 minutes. Using a slotted spoon, remove the tofu and place on a plate. Reserve the coconut milk.

Place the garlic, onion, dried chillies, lemon rind, ginger, spices and soy sauce in a blender or food processor and blend until a smooth paste is formed. Pour the remaining 150 ml/¼ pint coconut milk into a clean saucepan and whisk in the spicy paste. Cook, stirring continuously, for 15 minutes, or until the curry sauce is very thick.

Gradually whisk the reserved coconut milk into the curry and heat to simmering point. Add the cooked tofu and cook for 5–10 minutes. Blend the cornflour with 1 tablespoon of cold water and stir into the curry. Cook until thickened. Turn into a warmed serving dish and garnish with chilli, lemon wedges and coriander. Serve immediately with Thai fragrant rice.

Chicken Satay Salad

Serves 4

4 tbsp crunchy peanut butter
1 tbsp chilli sauce
1 garlic clove, peeled and crushed
2 tbsp cider vinegar
2 tbsp light soy sauce
2 tbsp dark soy sauce
2 tsp soft brown sugar
pinch salt
2 tsp freshly ground Sichuan peppercorns
450 g/1 lb dried egg noodles
2 tbsp sesame oil
1 tbsp groundnut oil
450 g/1 lb skinless, boneless chicken breast fillets, cut into cubes
shredded celery leaves, to garnish
cos lettuce, to serve

Place the peanut butter, chilli sauce, garlic, cider vinegar, soy sauces, sugar, salt and ground peppercorns in a food processor and blend to form a smooth paste. Scrape into a bowl, cover and chill in the refrigerator until required.

Bring a large saucepan of lightly salted water to the boil. Add the noodles and cook for 3–5 minutes. Drain and plunge into cold water. Drain again and toss in the sesame oil. Leave to cool.

Heat the wok until very hot, add the oil and when hot, add the chicken cubes. Stir-fry for 5–6 minutes until the chicken is golden brown and cooked through.

Remove the chicken from the wok using a slotted spoon and add to the noodles, together with the peanut sauce. Mix lightly together, then sprinkle with the shredded celery leaves and either serve immediately or leave until cold, then serve with cos lettuce.

Thai Rice Cakes with Mango Salsa

Serves 4

225 g/8 oz Thai fragrant rice
400 g can coconut milk
1 lemon grass stalk, bruised
2 kaffir lime leaves, shredded
1 tbsp vegetable oil, plus extra
for deep frying
1 garlic clove, peeled and
finely chopped
1 tsp freshly grated root ginger
1 red pepper, deseeded and
finely chopped
2 red chillies, deseeded and
finely chopped
1 medium egg, beaten
25 g/1 oz dried breadcrumbs

For the mango salsa:

1 large mango, peeled, stoned and
finely chopped
1 small red onion, peeled and
finely chopped
2 tbsp freshly chopped coriander
2 tbsp freshly chopped basil
juice of 1 lime

Wash the rice in several changes of water until the water stays relatively clear. Drain, place in a saucepan with a tight-fitting lid and add the coconut milk, lemon grass and lime leaves. Bring to the boil, cover and cook over the lowest possible heat for 10 minutes. Turn off the heat and leave to stand for 10 minutes, without lifting the lid.

Heat the wok, then add 1 tablespoon of oil and when hot, add the garlic, ginger, red pepper and half the chilli. Stir-fry for 1–2 minutes until just softened then place in a large bowl.

When the rice is cooked, turn into the mixing bowl and add the egg. Season to taste with salt and pepper and mix together well. Put the breadcrumbs into a shallow dish. Form the rice mixture into eight cakes and coat them in the breadcrumbs. Chill the cakes in the refrigerator for 30 minutes.

Meanwhile, make the mango salsa. In a bowl, mix together the mango, red onion, coriander, basil, lime juice and remaining red chilli and reserve.

Fill a clean wok about one third full of vegetable oil. Heat to 190°C/375°F, or until a cube of bread browns in 30 seconds. Cook the rice cakes, one or two at a time, for 2–3 minutes until golden and crisp. Drain on absorbent kitchen paper. Serve with the mango salsa.

Seafood Noodle Salad

Serves 4

8 baby squid, cleaned
2 tbsp mirin
2 tbsp rice vinegar
4 tbsp sunflower oil
1 red chilli, deseeded and
finely chopped
2 garlic cloves, peeled and crushed
6 spring onions, trimmed
and finely sliced
1 red pepper, deseeded and
finely sliced
1 tbsp turmeric
2 tsp ground coriander
8 raw tiger prawns, peeled
175 g/6 oz medium egg noodles
175 g/6 oz fresh white crabmeat
50 g/2 oz beansprouts
salt and freshly ground
black pepper

Remove the tentacles from the squid and reserve. Slit the squid bodies open down one side and open out flat.

Using a small sharp knife, score the flesh diagonally, first in one direction then the other, to make diamond shapes. Place in a bowl with the squid tentacles, mirin, rice vinegar, half the oil and the chilli and leave to marinate in the refrigerator for 1 hour.

Heat a wok until very hot. Add the remaining oil and, when hot, add the garlic, half the spring onions and the red pepper. Stir-fry for 1 minute, then add the turmeric and coriander. Cook for a further 30 seconds before adding the cleaned squid and its marinade and the prawns. Bring to the boil and simmer for 2–3 minutes, or until the squid and prawns are tender. Remove from the heat and leave to cool.

Cook the noodles for 3–4 minutes until tender, or according to packet directions. Drain well and put in a large serving bowl along with the white crabmeat and the cooled squid and prawn mixture. Stir together and leave until cold. Just before serving, add the beansprouts and remaining spring onions with seasoning to taste and serve.

Sweetcorn Fritters

Serves 4

4 tbsp groundnut oil
1 small onion, peeled and
finely chopped
1 red chilli, deseeded and
finely chopped
1 garlic clove, peeled and crushed
1 tsp ground coriander
325 g can sweetcorn
6 spring onions, trimmed and
finely sliced
1 medium egg, lightly beaten
salt and freshly ground
black pepper
3 tbsp plain flour
1 tsp baking powder
spring onion curls, to garnish
Thai-style chutney, to serve

Heat 1 tablespoon of the groundnut oil in a frying pan, add the onion and cook gently for 7–8 minutes or until beginning to soften. Add the chilli, garlic and ground coriander and cook for 1 minute, stirring continuously. Remove from the heat.

Drain the sweetcorn and tip into a mixing bowl. Lightly mash with a potato masher to break down the corn a little. Add the cooked onion mixture to the bowl with the spring onions and beaten egg. Season to taste with salt and pepper, then stir to mix together. Sift the flour and baking powder over the mixture and stir in.

Heat 2 tablespoons of the groundnut oil in a large frying pan. Drop four or five heaped teaspoonfuls of the sweetcorn mixture into the pan, and using a fish slice or spatula, flatten each to make a 1 cm/$^{1}/_{2}$ inch thick fritter.

Fry the fritters for 3 minutes, or until golden brown on the underside, turn over and fry for a further 3 minutes, or until cooked through and crisp.

Remove the fritters from the pan and drain on absorbent kitchen paper. Keep warm while cooking the remaining fritters, adding a little more oil if needed. Garnish with spring onion curls and serve immediately with a Thai-style chutney.

Oriental Noodle Peanut Salad with Coriander

Serves 4

350 g/12 oz rice vermicelli
1 litre/1³/₄ pints light chicken stock
2 tsp sesame oil
2 tbsp light soy sauce
8 spring onions
3 tbsp groundnut oil
2 hot green chillis, deseeded and thinly sliced
25 g/1 oz roughly chopped coriander
2 tbsp freshly chopped mint
125 g/4 oz cucumber, finely chopped
40 g/1¹/₂ oz beansprouts
40 g/1¹/₂ oz roasted peanuts, roughly chopped

Put the noodles into a large bowl. Bring the stock to the boil and immediately pour over the noodles. Leave to soak for 4 minutes, or according to the packet directions. Drain well, discarding the stock or saving it for another use. Mix together the sesame oil and soy sauce and pour over the hot noodles. Toss well to coat and leave until cold.

Trim and thinly slice 4 of the spring onions. Heat the oil in a wok over a low heat. Add the spring onions and, as soon as they sizzle, remove from the heat and leave to cool. When cold, toss with the noodles.

On a chopping board, cut the remaining spring onions lengthways 4–6 times, leave in a bowl of cold water until tassels form. Serve the noodles in individual bowls, each dressed with a little chilli, coriander, mint, cucumber, beansprouts and peanuts. Garnish with the spring onion tassels and serve.

Thai-style Cauliflower Potato Curry

Serves 4

450 g/1 lb new potatoes, peeled
and halved or quartered
350 g/12 oz cauliflower florets
3 garlic cloves, peeled and crushed
1 onion, peeled and finely chopped
40 g/1$\frac{1}{2}$ oz ground almonds
1 tsp ground coriander
$\frac{1}{2}$ tsp ground cumin
$\frac{1}{2}$ tsp turmeric
3 tbsp groundnut oil
salt and freshly ground black pepper
50 g/2 oz creamed coconut, broken
into small pieces
200 ml/7 fl oz vegetable stock
1 tbsp mango chutney
sprigs of fresh coriander, to garnish
freshly cooked long-grain rice,
to serve

Bring a saucepan of lightly salted water to the boil, add the potatoes and cook for 15 minutes or until just tender. Drain and leave to cool. Boil the cauliflower for 2 minutes, then drain and refresh under cold running water. Drain again and reserve.

Meanwhile, blend the garlic, onion, ground almonds and spices with 2 tablespoons of the oil and salt and pepper to taste in a food processor until a smooth paste is formed. Heat a wok, add the remaining oil and when hot, add the spice paste and cook for 3–4 minutes, stirring continuously.

Dissolve the creamed coconut in 6 tablespoons of boiling water and add to the wok. Pour in the stock, cook for 2–3 minutes, then stir in the cooked potatoes and cauliflower.

Stir in the mango chutney and heat through for 3–4 minutes or until piping hot. Tip into a warmed serving dish, garnish with sprigs of fresh coriander and serve immediately with freshly cooked rice.

Crispy Noodle Salad

Serves 4

2 tbsp sunflower seeds
2 tbsp pumpkin seeds
50 g/2 oz rice vermicelli or
stir-fry noodles
175 g/6 oz unsalted butter
2 tbsp sesame seeds,
lightly toasted
125 g/4 oz red cabbage, trimmed
and shredded
1 orange pepper, deseeded and
finely chopped
125 g/4 oz button mushrooms, wiped
and quartered
2 spring onions, trimmed and
finely chopped
salt and freshly ground black pepper
shredded pickled sushi ginger,
to garnish

Preheat the oven to 200°C/400°F/Gas Mark 6, then sprinkle the sunflower and pumpkin seeds on a baking sheet. Toast in the oven, stirring occasionally, for 10–15 minutes or until lightly toasted. Remove from the oven and leave to cool.

Crush the rice vermicelli into small pieces (this is easiest in a plastic bag or while the noodles are still in the packet), and reserve. Melt the butter in a small saucepan and leave to cool for a few minutes. Pour the clear yellow liquid carefully into a bowl, leaving behind the white milky solids. Discard the milky solids.

Heat the yellow, clarified butter in a wok and fry the crushed noodles in batches until browned, stirring constantly and gently. Remove the fried noodles as they cook, using a slotted spoon, and drain on absorbent kitchen paper. Transfer the noodles to a bowl and add the toasted seeds.

Mix together the red cabbage, orange pepper, button mushrooms and spring onions in a large bowl and season to taste with salt and pepper. Just before serving, add the noodles and seeds to the salad and mix gently. Garnish with a little sushi ginger and serve.

Cooked Vegetable Salad with Satay Sauce

Serves 4

125 ml/4 fl oz groundnut oil
225 g/8 oz unsalted peanuts
1 onion, peeled and finely chopped
1 garlic clove, peeled and crushed
¹/₂ tsp chilli powder
1 tsp ground coriander
¹/₂ tsp ground cumin
¹/₂ tsp sugar
1 tbsp dark soy sauce
2 tbsp fresh lemon juice
2 tbsp light olive oil
salt and freshly ground black pepper
125 g/4 oz French green beans, trimmed and halved
125 g/4 oz carrots
125 g/4 oz cauliflower florets
125 g/4 oz broccoli florets
125 g/4 oz Chinese leaves or pak choi, trimmed and shredded
125 g/4 oz beansprouts
1 tbsp sesame oil
sprigs fresh watercress and cucumber slivers, to garnish

Heat a wok, add the oil, and when hot, add the peanuts and stir-fry for 3–4 minutes. Drain on absorbent kitchen paper and leave to cool. Blend in a food processor to a fine powder.

Place the onion and garlic, with the spices, sugar, soy sauce, lemon juice and olive oil in a food processor. Season to taste with salt and pepper, then process into a paste. Transfer to a wok and stir-fry for 3–4 minutes.

Stir 600 ml/1 pint hot water into the paste and bring to the boil. Add the ground peanuts and simmer gently for 5–6 minutes or until the mixture thickens. Reserve the satay sauce.

Cook in batches in lightly salted boiling water. Cook the French beans, carrots, cauliflower and broccoli for 3–4 minutes, and the Chinese leaves or pak choi and beansprouts for 2 minutes. Drain each batch, drizzle over the sesame oil and arrange on a large warmed serving dish. Garnish with watercress sprigs and cucumber. Serve with the satay sauce.

Vegetables in Coconut Milk with Rice Noodles

Serves 4

75 g/3 oz creamed coconut
1 tsp salt
2 tbsp sunflower oil
2 garlic cloves, peeled and finely chopped
2 red peppers, deseeded and cut into thin strips
2.5 cm/1 inch piece of fresh root ginger, peeled and cut into thin strips
125 g/4 oz baby sweetcorn
2 tsp cornflour
2 medium ripe but still firm avocados
1 small Cos lettuce, cut into thick strips
freshly cooked rice noodles, to serve

Roughly chop the creamed coconut, place in a bowl with the salt, then pour over 600 ml/1 pint of boiling water. Stir until the coconut has dissolved completely and reserve.

Heat a wok or large frying pan, add the oil and when hot, add the chopped garlic, sliced peppers and ginger. Cook for 30 seconds, then cover and cook very gently for 10 minutes or until the peppers are soft.

Pour in the reserved coconut milk and bring to the boil. Stir in the baby sweetcorn, cover and simmer for 5 minutes. Blend the cornflour with 2 teaspoons of water, pour into the wok and cook, stirring, for 2 minutes or until thickened slightly.

Cut the avocados in half, peel, remove the stone and slice. Add to the wok with the lettuce strips and stir until well mixed and heated through. Serve immediately on a bed of rice noodles.

Thai Fried Noodles

Serves 4

450 g/1 lb tofu
2 tbsp dry sherry
125 g/4 oz medium egg noodles
125 g/4 oz mangetout, halved
3 tbsp groundnut oil
1 onion, peeled and finely sliced
1 garlic clove, peeled and
finely sliced
2.5 cm/1 inch piece fresh root
ginger, peeled and finely sliced
125 g/4 oz beansprouts
1 tbsp Thai fish sauce
2 tbsp light soy sauce
$\frac{1}{2}$ tsp sugar
salt and freshly ground
black pepper
$\frac{1}{2}$ courgette, cut into matchsticks

To garnish:

2 tbsp roasted peanuts,
roughly chopped
sprigs fresh basil

Cut the tofu into cubes and place in a bowl. Sprinkle over the sherry and toss to coat. Cover loosely and leave to marinate in the refrigerator for 30 minutes.

Bring a large saucepan of lightly salted water to the boil and add the noodles and mangetout. Simmer for 3 minutes or according to the packet instructions, then drain and rinse under cold running water. Leave to drain again.

Heat a wok or large frying pan, add the oil and when hot, add the onion and stir-fry for 2–3 minutes. Add the garlic and ginger and stir-fry for 30 seconds. Add the beansprouts and tofu, stir in the Thai fish sauce and the soy sauce with the sugar and season to taste with salt and pepper.

Stir-fry the tofu mixture over a medium heat for 2–3 minutes, then add the courgettes, noodles and mangetout and stir-fry for a further 1–2 minutes. Tip into a warmed serving dish or spoon on to individual plates. Sprinkle with the peanuts, add a sprig of basil and serve immediately.

Bean Cashew Stir Fry

Serves 4

3 tbsp sunflower oil

1 onion, peeled and finely chopped

1 celery stalk, trimmed and chopped

2.5 cm/1 inch piece fresh root
ginger, peeled and grated

2 garlic cloves, peeled and crushed

1 red chilli, deseeded and
finely chopped

175 g/6 oz fine French beans,
trimmed and halved

175 g/6 oz mangetout, sliced
diagonally into 3

75 g/3 oz unsalted cashew nuts

1 tsp brown sugar

125 ml/4 fl oz vegetable stock

2 tbsp dry sherry

1 tbsp light soy sauce

1 tsp red wine vinegar

salt and freshly ground black pepper

freshly chopped coriander,
to garnish

Heat a wok or large frying pan, add the oil and when hot, add the onion and celery and stir-fry gently for 3–4 minutes or until softened.

Add the ginger, garlic and chilli to the wok and stir-fry for 30 seconds. Stir in the French beans and mangetout together with the cashew nuts and continue to stir-fry for 1–2 minutes, or until the nuts are golden brown.

Dissolve the sugar in the stock, then blend with the sherry, soy sauce and vinegar. Stir into the bean mixture and bring to the boil. Simmer gently, stirring occasionally for 3–4 minutes, or until the beans and mangetout are tender but still crisp and the sauce has thickened slightly. Season to taste with salt and pepper. Transfer to a warmed serving bowl or spoon on to individual plates. Sprinkle with freshly chopped coriander and serve immediately.

Thai Noodles & Vegetables with Tofu

Serves 4

225 g/8 oz firm tofu
2 tbsp soy sauce
zest of 1 lime, grated
2 lemon grass stalks
1 red chilli
1 litre/1¾ pint vegetable stock
2 slices fresh root ginger, peeled
2 garlic cloves, peeled
2 sprigs of fresh coriander
175 g/6 oz dried thread egg noodles
125 g/4 oz shiitake or button
mushrooms, sliced if large
2 carrots, peeled and
cut into matchsticks
125 g/4 oz mangetout
125 g/4 oz bok choy or other
Chinese leaf
1 tbsp freshly chopped coriander
salt and freshly ground black pepper
coriander sprigs, to garnish

Drain the tofu well and cut into cubes. Put into a shallow dish with the soy sauce and lime rind. Stir well to coat and leave to marinate for 30 minutes.

Meanwhile, put the lemon grass and chilli on a chopping board and bruise with the side of a large knife, ensuring the blade is pointing away from you. Put the vegetable stock in a large saucepan and add the lemon grass, chilli, ginger, garlic, and coriander. Bring to the boil, cover and simmer gently for 20 minutes.

Strain the stock into a clean pan. Return to the boil and add the noodles, tofu and its marinade and the mushrooms. Simmer gently for 4 minutes.

Add the carrots, mangetout, bok choy, coriander and simmer for a further 3–4 minutes until the vegetables are just tender. Season to taste with salt and pepper. Garnish with coriander sprigs. Serve immediately.

Indonesian Salad with Peanut Dressing

Serves 4

225 g/8 oz new potatoes, scrubbed
1 large carrot, peeled and cut into matchsticks
125 g/4 oz French beans, trimmed
225 g/8 oz tiny cauliflower florets
125 g/4 oz cucumber, cut into matchsticks
75 g/3 oz fresh bean sprouts
3 medium eggs, hard-boiled and quartered

For the peanut dressing:

2 tbsp sesame oil
1 garlic clove, peeled and crushed
1 red chilli, deseeded and finely chopped
150 g/5 oz crunchy peanut butter
6 tbsp hot vegetable stock
2 tsp soft light brown sugar
2 tsp dark soy sauce
1 tbsp lime juice

Cook the potatoes in a saucepan of boiling salted water for 15–20 minutes until tender. Remove with a slotted spoon and thickly slice into a large bowl. Keep the saucepan of water boiling.

Add the carrot, French beans and cauliflower to the water, return to the boil and cook for 2 minutes, or until just tender. Drain and refresh under cold running water, then drain well. Add to the potatoes with the cucumber and bean sprouts.

To make the dressing, gently heat the sesame oil in a small saucepan. Add the garlic and chilli and cook for a few seconds, then remove from the heat. Stir in the peanut butter.

Stir in the stock, a little at a time. Add the remaining ingredients and mix together to make a thick, creamy dressing.

Divide the vegetables between four plates and arrange the eggs on top. Drizzle the dressing over the salad and serve immediately.

Pad Thai Noodles
with Mushrooms

Serves 4

125 g/4 oz flat rice noodles
or rice vermicelli
1 tbsp vegetable oil
2 garlic cloves, peeled
and finely chopped
1 medium egg, lightly beaten
225 g/8 oz mixed mushrooms,
including shiitake, oyster, field,
brown and wild mushrooms
2 tbsp lemon juice
1¹/₂ tbsp Thai fish sauce
¹/₂ tsp sugar
¹/₂ tsp cayenne pepper
2 spring onions, trimmed and cut
into 2.5 cm/1 inch pieces
50 g/2 oz fresh beansprouts

To garnish:

chopped roasted peanuts
freshly chopped coriander

Cook the noodles according to the packet instructions. Drain well and reserve.

Heat a wok or large frying pan. Add the oil and garlic. Fry until just golden. Add the egg and stir quickly to break it up.

Cook for a few seconds before adding the noodles and mushrooms. Scrape down the sides of the pan to ensure they mix with the egg and garlic.

Add the lemon juice, fish sauce, sugar, cayenne pepper, spring onions and half of the beansprouts, stirring quickly all the time.

Cook over a high heat for a further 2–3 minutes until everything is heated through.

Turn on to a serving plate. Top with the remaining beansprouts. Garnish with the chopped roasted peanuts and fresh coriander and serve immediately.

Stir-fried Greens

Serves 4

450 g/1 lb Chinese leaves
225 g/8 oz pak choi
225 g/8 oz broccoli florets
1 tbsp sesame seeds
1 tbsp groundnut oil
1 tbsp fresh root ginger, peeled
and finely chopped
3 garlic cloves, peeled and
finely chopped
2 red chillies, deseeded and
split in half
50 ml/2 fl oz chicken stock
2 tbsp Chinese rice wine
1 tbsp dark soy sauce
1 tsp light soy sauce
2 tsp black bean sauce
freshly ground black pepper
2 tsp sugar
1 tsp sesame oil

Separate the Chinese leaves and pak choi and wash well. Cut into 2.5 cm/1 inch strips. Separate the broccoli into small florets. Heat a wok or large frying pan, add the sesame seeds and stir-fry for 30 seconds or until browned.

Add the oil to the wok and when hot, add the ginger, garlic and chillies and stir-fry for 30 seconds. Add the broccoli and stir-fry for 1 minute. Add the Chinese leaves and pak choi and stir-fry for a further 1 minute.

Pour the chicken stock and Chinese rice wine into the wok with the soy and black bean sauces. Season to taste with pepper and add the sugar. Reduce the heat and simmer for 6–8 minutes, or until the vegetables are tender but still firm to the bite. Tip into a warmed serving dish, removing the chillies if preferred. Drizzle with the sesame oil and serve immediately.

Thai Stuffed Eggs with Spinach Sesame Seeds

Makes 8

4 large eggs
salt and freshly ground black pepper
225 g/8 oz baby spinach
2 garlic cloves, peeled and crushed
1 tbsp spring onions, trimmed and finely chopped
1 tbsp sesame seeds
75 g/3 oz plain flour
1 tbsp light olive oil
300 ml/½ pint vegetable oil for frying

To garnish:

sliced red chilli
snipped fresh chives

Bring a small saucepan of water to the boil, add the eggs, bring back to the boil and cook for 6–7 minutes. Plunge into cold water, then shell and cut in half lengthways. Using a teaspoon, remove the yolks and place in a bowl. Reserve the whites.

Place 1 teaspoon of water and ½ teaspoon of salt in a saucepan, add the spinach and cook until tender and wilted. Drain, squeeze out the excess moisture and chop. Mix with the egg yolk, then stir in the garlic, spring onions and sesame seeds. Season to taste with salt and pepper. Fill the egg shells with the mixture, smoothing into a mound.

Place the flour in a bowl with the olive oil, a large pinch of salt and 125 ml/4 fl oz warm water. Beat together to make completely smooth batter.

Heat a wok, add the vegetable oil and heat to 180°C/350°F. Dip the stuffed eggs in the batter, allowing any excess batter to drip back into the bowl, and deep-fry in batches for 3–4 minutes or until golden brown. Place the eggs in the wok filled side down first, then turn over to finish cooking. Remove from the wok with a slotted spoon and drain on absorbent kitchen paper. Serve hot or cold garnished with snipped chives and chilli rings.

Sweetcorn Cakes

Serves 6–8

250 g/9 oz self-raising flour
3 tbsp Thai red curry paste
2 tbsp light soy sauce
2 tsp sugar
2 kaffir lime leaves, finely shredded
12 fine French beans, trimmed, finely chopped and blanched
340 g can sweetcorn, drained
salt and freshly ground black pepper
2 medium eggs
50 g/2 oz fresh white breadcrumbs
vegetable oil for deep-frying

For the dipping sauce:

2 tbsp hoisin sauce
1 tbsp soft light brown sugar
1 tbsp sesame oil

To serve:

halved cucumber slices
spring onions, sliced diagonally

Place the flour in a bowl, make a well in the centre, then add the curry paste, soy sauce and the sugar together with the shredded kaffir lime leaves, French beans and sweetcorn. Season to taste with salt and pepper, then beat 1 of the eggs and add to the mixture. Stir in with a fork adding 1–2 tablespoons of cold water to form a stiff dough. Knead lightly on a floured surface and form into a ball.

Divide the mixture into 16 pieces and shape into small balls, then flatten to form cakes about 1 cm/^{1}/$_2$ inch thick and 7.5 cm/3 inches in diameter. Beat the remaining egg and pour into a shallow dish. Dip the cakes first in a little beaten egg, then in the breadcrumbs until lightly coated.

Heat the oil in either a wok or deep-fat fryer to 180°C/350°F and deep-fry the cakes for 2–3 minutes or until golden brown in colour. Using a slotted spoon, remove and drain on absorbent kitchen paper.

Meanwhile, blend the hoisin sauce, sugar, 1 tablespoon of water and the sesame oil together until smooth and pour into a small bowl. Serve immediately with the sweetcorn cakes, cucumber and spring onions.

Warm Lobster Salad
with Hot Thai Dressing

Serves 4

1 orange
50 g/2 oz granulated sugar
2 Cos lettuce hearts, shredded
1 small avocado, peeled and sliced
1/2 cucumber, peeled and sliced
1 mango, peeled, stoned and sliced
1 tbsp butter or vegetable oil
1 large lobster, meat removed and
cut into bite-sized pieces
2 tbsp Thai or Italian basil leaves
4 large cooked prawns, peeled
with tails left on, to garnish

For the dressing:
1 tbsp vegetable oil
4–6 spring onions, trimmed and
sliced into 5 cm/2 inch pieces
2.5 cm/1 inch piece fresh root
ginger, peeled and grated
1 garlic clove, peeled and crushed
zest of 1 lime and juice of 2–3 limes
2 tbsp Thai fish sauce; 1 tbsp brown
sugar; 1–2 tsp sweet chilli sauce
1 tbsp sesame oil

With a sharp knife, cut the orange rind into thin julienne strips, then cook in boiling water for 2 minutes.

Drain the orange strips, then plunge into cold running water, drain and return to the saucepan with the sugar and 1 cm/1/2 inch water. Simmer until soft, then add 1 tablespoon of cold water to stop cooking. Remove from the heat and reserve. Arrange the lettuce on four large plates and arrange the avocado, cucumber and mango slices over the lettuce.

Heat a wok or large frying pan, add the butter or oil and when hot, but not sizzling, add the lobster and stir-fry for 1–2 minutes or until heated through. Remove and drain on absorbent kitchen paper.

To make the dressing, heat the vegetable oil in a wok, then add the spring onions, ginger and garlic and stir-fry for 1 minute. Add the lime zest, lime juice, fish sauce, sugar and chilli sauce. Stir until the sugar dissolves. Remove from the heat, add the sesame oil with the orange rind and liquor.

Arrange the lobster meat over the salad and drizzle with dressing. Sprinkle with basil leaves, garnish with prawns and serve immediately.

Chinese Egg Fried Rice

Serves 4

250 g/9 oz long-grain rice
1 tbsp dark sesame oil
2 large eggs
1 tbsp sunflower oil
2 garlic cloves, peeled and crushed
2.5 cm/1 inch piece fresh root ginger, peeled and grated
1 carrot, peeled and cut into matchsticks
125 g/4 oz mangetout, halved
220 g can water chestnuts, drained and halved
1 yellow pepper, deseeded and diced
4 spring onions, trimmed and finely shredded
2 tbsp light soy sauce
$^{1}/_{2}$ tsp paprika
salt and freshly ground black pepper

Bring a saucepan of lightly salted water to the boil, add the rice and cook for 15 minutes or according to the packet instructions. Drain and leave to cool.

Heat a wok or large frying pan and add the sesame oil. Beat the eggs in a small bowl and pour into the hot wok. Using a fork, draw the egg in from the sides of the pan to the centre until it sets, then turn over and cook the other side. When set and golden turn out on to a board. Leave to cool, then cut into very thin strips.

Wipe the wok clean with absorbent kitchen paper, return to the heat and add the sunflower oil. When hot add the garlic and ginger and stir-fry for 30 seconds. Add the remaining vegetables and continue to stir-fry for 3–4 minutes, or until tender but still crisp.

Stir the reserved cooked rice into the wok with the soy sauce and paprika and season to taste with salt and pepper. Fold in the cooked egg strips and heat through. Tip into a warmed serving dish and serve immediately.

Index

Index